LIFE MASTERY PROCESS

A BOOK FOR THE OPEN-MINDED

Phil:

Congrats on All your success!
Take care.

Life Mastery Process

A BOOK FOR THE OPEN-MINDED

by W. Alan Gay

Chartered Financial Consultant
Certified Financial Planner

CAK Publishing _____
PO Box 953   Broomfield, CO 80038

Published by CAK Publishing, PO Box 953, Broomfield, CO 80038

Printed by McNaughton-Gunn, Inc., Saline MI, USA

I dedicate this book to

My beloved wife Liz

who makes it all worthwhile

and

My devoted dog Hosehead

who saw me through my darkest times

*** DISCLAIMER ***

The material in this book is not intended to substitute for actual financial planning credentials, such as Chartered Financial Consultant (ChFC) or Certified Financial Planner (CFP). Changes in your financial strategy should only be attempted with the advice of your own personal financial planner, attorney, and tax advisor. While every effort has been made to make the information in this book correct, the contents are not guaranteed to be (or remain) correct, especially the tax information (which changes, on the average, every eight months). This book is designed to aid you in identifying financial possibilities, and is not intended to be used as the sole reference for making any financial decision.

Table of Contents

THE LIFE MASTERY PROCESS

A BOOK FOR THE OPEN-MINDED

— — — — — —

FOREWORD

We could look at the financial services industry as likely one of the most difficult businesses in which to succeed. We could say that, within the business world, the lessons learned in mastering financial services could be applied to any business.

Polls tell us that 73% of single people worry about their finances. And married people? In the United States, one in two marriages end in divorce. According to a Gallup Poll in which participants were asked the reason for the divorce, 93% replied that it had to do with finances: attitude toward saving, budget, overspending or other concern about money. Obviously, finances are of key importance to everyone.

In this book you will learn a method that gives you the best chance to succeed financially. In fact, you will learn more than you need to know to simply do the family finances. This book has the potential to train you to be a financial planner. This will help you to understand what to discuss with your planner (if you choose to use one), and what questions to ask relative to any financial product. With the knowledge you can gain, you may never again have to worry about money!

I really liked the part in the movie *Forrest Gump* where he and Lt. Taylor had purchased a fruit company called Apple Computer. Forrest said that, "Now we never have to worry about money again, and that is a good thing!" See – even Forrest Gump worried about money.

I had the pleasure of serving our great country for twenty years, four years on active duty and the rest in active reserve. What did I like best about the military? How they trained me for one level higher than I actually needed, making me super-qualified to complete my tasks. When it came time for me to perform, that extra training insured that I would succeed. I ended up completing my tasks with little stress, since my extra skills made it less difficult.

I have designed this book to over-train you. Depending on your current skill with investing, this book can help you in different ways. If you struggle with things financial, it can aid you in understanding investments. If you are adept with your own family finances, this can help you plan for your retirement. If the business of financial planning excites you, this could lead you into a new career. For everyone, this book can make it easier to work with a financial planner, or to do the work yourself. In either case, you can make more educated choices after absorbing the material contained here.

The method covered in here is truly unusual and unique. Here you will learn how to be a financial planner. Many of you may ask, "Why would I want to be a financial planner?" You may not like dealing with finances, even your own. However, you must deal with them in some fashion. Even if you hire a financial planner, you must still be able to monitor their results. More importantly, you must direct him or her on how to invest your money. Do you want an aggressive portfolio, or a more conservative one? What level of risk are you willing to take? You need to have questions (and answers) prepared for that person so that they can make the best possible financial decisions for you and your family.

For a good example, consider the annuity option available in most government and many corporate retirement plans. Depending on the program you choose, you could retire with 20-34% more income than someone who elects guaranteed annuity options. Another plan offers 80% more income, which you could obtain by giving up only a few minor advantage and guarantees.

Now that you have made the decision to become a planner (even if it's only for your own money), I suggest that you dedicate yourself to becoming one of the best! Why would anyone pursue any career that they could not both excel at and become excited about? (See the section called Hakuna Matata, a Swahili phrase taken from the popular Disney movie, *Lion King*. The phrase means, "No worries for the rest of your days.") If you are excellent at and excited about your work, then you are in the right place. You are a leader and your work will always be your play. You have an excellent opportunity to maximize your human potential and truly enjoy your life.

This book will give you a great plan for succeeding in the financial services industry. However, there are many ways to succeed. You can use our method as a road map, then chart your own detours – take away what doesn't work for you, add what does. For me, it was very exciting to realize that the secrets of success in becoming a great planner could be applied to handling my own finances. The things you learn here may lead to a great relationship with a wonderful planner whom you hire for your own family finances. Even if you do not become a planner, you still will benefit by knowing what really is relevant for success in the financial world.

Ask yourself this question: "What things interest me financially and what can I really get excited about?" If you can answer, "A sound financial future," then you should have great confidence that you are right on track with this book.

But what if you have decided to be a financial planner? First, I commend you on your courage! Even though you are entering into a business where only 1 in 296 succeed (LIMRA study), I can promise you that you will never regret your decision. Whether you succeed or fail, you will grow into a much stronger and enlightened individual. Some of the strongest people I have met were people in the financial services industry. I predict you will always look back on a career as a planner as a great time of learning and challenge. I can assure you that your life will be more exciting than ever.

Within these pages you will learn how to become the most successful financial planner, life insurance salesman and securities broker in your realm. Your name may become synonymous with financial success locally! Many of the concepts given here simply involve setting proper habits. You can apply this process to other small businesses. By setting up new habits, you can make a tremendous difference in your life and move ahead financially.

My favorite part of the Optimist Creed is the line, "Make yourself so strong that no one can disturb your piece of mind." Once we get our financial life in order, we can then pay full attention to the other four areas of our lives. (I have reserved chapter 3 to describe the five areas of life, and discuss their importance.) If you can achieve success in all areas of your life, you are an extraordinary individual.

HOW TO USE THIS BOOK

Each chapter explores a new principal or concept. Some of the information is technical, some philosophical. Try to master each step given before you go to the next. Each chapter is built on the previous. If you have difficulty mastering a particular chapter, just read and reread until the concept is yours.

I suggest you not move to a new chapter until you complete the exercises and you have an implicit understanding of the concept presented. Sometimes, you may feel uneasy with a concept, with applying it in your life. This may be due to things in your past influencing your state of mind. That's okay! Whether or not you choose to apply that concept, you should still be aware of it and how it fits into your progress. Once again, you can achieve your overall objective by simply mastering one chapter at a time.

So rather than reading the whole book in one sitting, stop and do the exercises at the end of each chapter. Many of the concepts may go totally against your idea of the correct and proper way to do things. As a result, some concepts will be particularly challenging to adopt. That is why I sub-titled this <u>A Book for the Open-Minded</u>. You must have an open mind to read and benefit from this book.

With this book, I challenge you to adopt a new learning strategy. Over the years, I have had many people ask me why I took a particular class. They say, "You know most of that, you have taken classes like that before." I tell them that if I could get just one or two good ideas out of the class, it could make a big difference in my life.

Somehow these people think that every concept in a class or book must be new, relevant and usable in their life for them to benefit. However, I have found that at least 10% of every class I've ever taken is useful and appropriate to my life. Sometimes this 10% has made a giant difference. Other people who have adopted this mind set have discovered the same thing. Just remember: this 10% can make you or save you thousands of dollars. It can make you an expert in your field and give you the confidence to make great decisions in your life.

This book, I assure you, is one of those books that can make a difference for you. I believe this, and I hope sincerely that it does help you. However, you have to apply what you learn in these pages.

I think you will find this book full of practical information that you can use, and that it will compare well to any college class you have taken.

Who knows? This course could change your life. If you approach it with an open mind, you should find a wealth of useful information. If you can maintain that open mind beyond this course, you will be years ahead of your peers and open to a lifetime of learning and possibilities. I believe people can always benefit from learning, whether from books or in classroom situations. It will keep you sharp and constantly improving, and make yourself more valuable to others.

My wish for you is that your hopes and dreams come true. I hope that your goals and values are yours as well. Most of all, if your dream is to become a financial planner, I hope more than anything that this book helps you to achieve it!

In this book from time to time I will identify critical, major and minor errors. These errors are defined as follows:

Critical Errors – Mistakes that renders the final results unachievable. These errors merit your attention because they keep you from your objective despite any amount of effort or energy.

Major Errors – A mistake which makes reaching your final objective possible, but with greatly increased effort or energy required.

Minor Errors – A mistake which slows down the progress to your final result. These errors are very common and reduce your efficiency on the path to your goal.

CRITICAL ERROR: Using what you have learned in the past, or relying on conventional wisdom, to live your life in the future. Conventional wisdom is dangerous! It is the guarantee of a mediocre life. Try to live your life 'out of the box'.

CHAPTER 1

BUSINESS IS POURING IN AND WE ARE NOT SURE WHY!

A wise man once started in business after receiving a 'small' inheritance of less than $100,000. With that principal as his seed money, he quickly doubled, then quadrupled his money, then increased it tenfold. In only ten and a half years, he turned the money into a fortune so large that he knew he could never live long enough to give it all away, even if he tried. His net worth was a staggering $1.1 billion dollars! He had discovered a business principle that insured his success:

Find out what must happen in a business agreement for all parties to feel like it's a good deal, and then give the other party even more.

How does that work, you might ask? With a simple example we can see the mechanics at work. Keep in mind, though, that the most important effect goes on 'behind the scenes'.

Let us look at a real estate deal. Imagine you are the first party, who is putting up the money. Call the second party Mike, who will perform the manual labor in this deal. After careful negotiation you both agree that to make this transaction a win-win situation, you will split the profits 50-50. Just before singing the contract, with all the attorneys in the room, you announce, "I would like to change the contract." After the anger subsides and a few comments are made such as, "You gave us your word," politely state that you wish to give 60% of the profit to Mike, with 40% going to you. The reason for the change is simple: "I want to make sure that Mike gets a good deal."

Then throw fuel on the fire and create a unforgettable moment in your life and business by saying, "Mike, you are my good and trusted friend. I want to make certain that you come out ahead here. Will the new 60-40 split satisfy you?"

Get ready! Most of the people at the table will fall out of their chairs in shock. Most attorneys have learned to take all they can from each transaction, and this concept violates everything they understand. You may hear them say, "In my entire fifty years in law, I have never seen anything like this." In fact, when the attorney gets back to her office she will share with all her co-workers (including the partners) what just happened. They will likely be equally shocked.

When Mike gets home, he will share this extraordinary event first with his wife, then his colleagues, his neighbors, his dog, and everyone else he knows. Before you know it, people will be saying things behind your back like, "He cares more about me than himself!" Soon people will call to meet you, hoping to do business with you. Rats! Don't you hate it when that happens? Now you have to hire more staff to process your deals. You may need an extra employee just to take your paychecks to the bank.

It seems just too simple, doesn't it?

Now can you accept a couple of these facts?

You can never take more from life than it will take from you. In fact, if you take too much, you will find yourself bankrupt in some or all of the five areas of your life (see Chapter 3 for a discussion of the five areas). On the other hand, the success that you share with others will always come back to enrich your life.

You can never give more to life than it will return to you. Life is very large. Life will open up its abundance and pour out more than you can store. Life is exactly like God, isn't it? Let us look at a few references: Koran, Sura 2, verse 117: "It is righteousness to love God and practice regular charity. To give of your substance out of love for Him to orphans and the poor." If you are influenced more by the Gautama, Siddhartha and Buddhism, "The philosopher is wise who gives – the philosopher has more because he gives." The Christian and Jewish scripture are more to the point. The Prophet Malachi called the Jews 'Robbers' if they did not bring the full tithe into the storehouse. If they did, Malachi promised, and "Put the Lord to the Test," He would "open the windows of Heaven and pour out an overflowing blessing. Their granaries would not be able to hold it all. He would rebuke the devourer in the field for them. Their vines would cast fourth fruit before it was ripe and he would heal their land!" In the Christian Scriptures, Luke 6:38 promises that the Giver will receive, "Full measure, shaken together and running over, will men pour into your lap."

Sadly, most people react the opposite way, trying to suck all they can out of each deal. They enter agreements that provide marginal benefits to the other person. When the deal is in progress, they try to squeeze even more from the contract. Then, when they are done, they draw the last bit of life from it. If that is not enough, they then hire an attorney to try to get a little more. The other party to the transaction can't wait for the deal to end, vowing never to deal with that person again.

In today's fast-paced, hard-spending world, generosity is a hard concept to swallow! We are taught to 'look out for number one', and that the world is out to get you. However, if you treat others in this fashion, they will naturally tend to treat you in the same fashion.

Sometimes, when things don't work out in our life, we say, "I just hit a bit of bad luck." In reality, we usually know when we do not deserve the blessing of life. I find it sad that so few people own up to this, choosing instead to live their life in denial. A person is truly mature when they take full responsibility for the successes and failures in their life. If you have trouble doing this, try an affirmation: When you get up in the morning, say, "I am responsible for my life." When things are not working out, say, "I am responsible". Whatever happens, you will feel a great solace that you have taken responsibility for yourself.

Please! Do everything you can to not operate in the mode of greed. Do not look upon every deal as an opportunity to 'beat' someone else in business. Do not enter into lawsuits, but allow life – and God – to sort that out. Spend your energy on things that benefit your family and others.

Exercises

1. Identify all agreements where you could use this strategy. Write to me and tell me your most exciting breakthrough in this area. I love good stories!

2. Identify, in writing, agreements where you did not use this strategy, but can now alter the agreement. It could possibly be done at the end of the agreement.

3. Who are the individuals or businesses who could benefit from your product or service and with whom you might enter into agreements like this? A long-term relationship with these people could make a difference in your life now and in the future. Give these contacts additional consideration and energy.

4. What must happen for you to take responsibility in all areas of your life? Write down something in each of the five areas of your life: financial; spiritual; health; friendships; inner peace.

What does 'generosity' have to do with the securities, insurance, retirement or estate planning business? In these businesses, you cannot change the compensation when you work with clients. Even though you may not rebate commissions, you can do other things to give back more value.

Do something that your client values, something he doesn't expect! For example, find out the client's favorite charity, and give them a gift on his behalf . To discover what might please your clients, ask them to fill out a survey. You might also use a marketing or research company to get other ideas. Do not be confused by the fact that the clients first came to you to get a good return on their money, or for help with their estate or retirement planning. Make sure you deliver those services first before going the extra mile. After all, any good will you generate could be destroyed if you don't deliver what you originally promised. Let the client know that you want to make sure this relationship or transaction is a good deal for them.

Additional Commentary

One financial genius once said, "For a young man to be successful, all he needs to do is simply save 10% of all he earns and buy real estate in his town near the edge of the town." He reasoned that if the person owned land at the city's edge, he could develop it with money he'd saved, or sell it to boost his savings. Thus, you might choose to get involved in real estate transactions, remembering to alter the agreements as indicated in this chapter.

Real estate deals are perfect ones in which to change agreements and make friends for life. You may enjoy being a legend known for your superb business dealings, making sure everyone wins.

If your business uses agreements on a regular basis, this strategy will be very easy to use. The key is to first list all of the transactions that now use agreements. Next, write three to five ways that you could alter the transaction. Next, talk to the other party in the agreement and try to figure out what they would value most from your list. Here are some possibilities:

♦ Give a higher percentage of money back. (Do the project for less cost). Refund some of the money and tell her you had some additional discounts that you were able to pass on to her and you wanted to make sure she got a good deal.
♦ Give a free additional service such as a gift to her children or charity in her name.
♦ Give additional material or workmanship.

♦ Give a plaque or a memorial in their name. One deck builder put a plaque with a prayer on it and a dedication to the family. The prayer said, "May the sun that touches each occupant warm the bones and the soul of all who use this deck. May each person present feel and radiate warmth and love. May each person who sits in the hot tub, attends a barbecue or sets foot on this deck be blessed and protected. May each person who is present feel love and be genuinely appreciated for just exactly the miracle of God that they are. May the family look on this special place as the family circle of safety, happiness and a sanctuary of love."

♦ Refer some other business to them for doing business with you.

The key is to find what they value and give it to them as an extra they were not expecting. Do this by picking the best one off the list. Remember not to 'give away the shop'. We must make a profit, but by slightly decreasing your profit you can make a giant impact in this transaction. Treat your products and services as experiences!

If you have already entered into agreements and those agreements have not yet paid out but will soon settle, do the same thing. This will likely create even more shock than changing the deal at the beginning. It can be extremely effective. A deal or transaction that is altered at the end is even more surprising, and can be a tremendous crowd pleaser. Very often you can do this without the attorneys redoing all the contracts. Often people who have mastered this technique wait until the end of the transaction to alter it.

Go back and find out what they value and give it to them.

If you have a chance of repeat business with this customer then this is a must!

Write down the greatest opportunities that you have and match that with your capability. When entering into a transaction, rate from 1 to 10 the value of the opportunity. Then ask, on a scale of 1 to 10, how capable are you (or your organization) to deal with this opportunity. For example, say you own a widget factory that can produce up to 5000 widgets per month if you go to 24-hour/day production. Typically, your customers order 200 widgets (an opportunity ranking of 3, capability of 10). One day a new customer inquires about an order of 10,000 widgets, with a potential profit of $150,000. Rate this opportunity as 10, but your capability only comes in at 5, since you can only offer 1000 widgets before putting off your other orders and running non-stop production.

It is in your best interest, before you enter into the transaction, to compare your opportunity with your capability to determine your chances for favorable results. Let us look at some examples:

Example 1: The opportunity is rated at 10 and capability is rated at 4. Suggestion: Do not enter into an agreement or transaction since the results the client receives may be less than they expected. This could spell disaster for the client, and the chance of referrals would be very low. In fact, very possibly the client could say negative things about your product or service, which is the opposite of what we are trying to achieve.

Example 2: The opportunity is rated at 3 and capability is rated at 9. Suggestion: Do not enter into an agreement, since you are likely to be underpaid for your time and effort. You may not be committed to the service or final outcome for the client. (You might be bored by the lack of challenge.) The final result may again be an unhappy client.

Example 3: The opportunity is rated at 6 and capability is rated at 5. Congratulations! This is just the type of situation you were looking for. First, you will indeed be compensated for your service. Next, you will be challenged by this transaction. Also, you will likely be able to deliver a quality or service to the client. When this situation exists, simply apply the other principles in this chapter.

Other Exercises

Keep a sheet of paper at your desk. On that sheet mark a scale of 1 to 10 for each new client. On that scale, rate the client for opportunity and your organization for capability. If you just started your company, you may be a one or two person shop, and so your capability is the capability of the organization.

Finally, make a conscious decision about each client. Will your needs and the client's needs be met when you compare capability to the opportunity? Don't forget to add into the client's opportunity score the chance for referrals. Would you consider entering into a deal and forgoing a reasonable compensation in order to cement a relationship and possibly score a referral later on?

The question always comes up, "What if this is the last (or only) transaction I will ever do with this person, and we both know it?" I still suggest you alter the agreement and make it a good deal for the other party past the point they expect. You would be shocked at how small this planet is, and how that person might just share the story of your transaction with someone who really has money. Their enthusiasm may infect the other person, turning them into clients. They might call you and beg you do business with them. Then there we are, back to more large paychecks again.

Okay, so the above are just stories. Now let us look at one actual example of how this worked, with an eye towards applying this in our business. Do not overlook the example of the person who turned his $100,000 into an unimaginable fortune.

Years ago, I had a real estate transaction with my good friend Willie Kellum in Denver, Colorado. Willie was purchasing a duplex in Denver. Having little money at the time, I asked him if I could participate in the transaction, knowing that he would not benefit from my small amount of money. He said, "Alan, I will help anyone who will help himself." Seven months later he called me and told me the deal was done and for me to come and get my money. I had invested $4,000 with him. I walked into his store and he handed me a check for $9,125! I was shocked! I had expected to get about $5,500 at the very most. I took $1,000 out to pay bills and reinvested the other money with Mr. Kellum.

During the next three years, I told every single client that was interested in real estate about Mr. Kellum. Many went on to join Willie in other business deals. About two years later I did business with Willie again on a handshake basis. I gave him $850,000 to use in one real estate deal. When the deal closed, Mr. Kellum made millions of dollars, and I enjoyed a return of over 40%. Do you think he got his money back from the smaller deals he had let me in on?

How quickly can you get this into your life? If you can do this, you will benefit far beyond your expectations.

CHAPTER 2

THE TAX FREE SOLUTION

Wouldn't you love to have tax-free money at retirement? *Fat chance,* you're probably thinking. I'm sure you've heard that, except for gains drawn from a Roth IRA, no income is ever tax-free. Or could it be? In this chapter, you will learn how to grow your money into a tax-free treasure. The benefits of this program will amaze you.

Let's start with a cardinal rule of financial planning: always show your client *how* to fund his financial future. Sky-high taxes already rob them of much of their income, and television (the great financial wrecking ball) encourages them to spend the rest. Too many people live at or beyond their means, leaving little money for savings. Studies done in 1998 show that television causes (or at least aids) an increase in debt and lifestyle. This study tracked individuals who had lived very frugally in a less developed country before moving to the United States. After ten years, the typical person had significantly increased their debt burden. These individuals blamed spending habits learned from television.

MAJOR ERROR: Not setting up a plan to provide tax-free money at retirement. Tax-free means income tax free, estate tax free and social security received free of income tax.

One of the best places for clients to find money is to look at a qualified plan: an IRA, 401(k), 403(b), Profit Sharing Plan, Money Purchase Plan, SEP Plan or Simple IRA. These plans allow for different size deposits and deductions, but they are taxed the same way: The money put into the plan is tax-deductible, the money grows tax deferred, but it is fully taxable when you withdraw the funds. In addition, any distribution from a qualified plan is normally subject to a 10% penalty if the owner of the plan is less than age 59½.

One way you *can* pull money from a qualified plan is by using IRS rule 72(t). This special section of the internal revenue code allows a person to take money from their qualified plan while avoiding the 10% early withdrawal penalty. The object is to transfer the money from the qualified plan into a fund that will grow tax-deferred and provide tax-free money at retirement.

Let us look at an example and at the vehicle which can give us this tax-free money at retirement. In our example, Bob starts with $100,000, which he had accumulated in his 401(k). Bob left his employer and rolled the money into an IRA to avoid paying the taxes on his 401(k) withdrawal. The rules for this transaction are simple; the money must be directly rolled from the 401(k) to the IRA with only the plan custodian (plan caretakers) touching the money. If Bob handles the money, then 20% of the distribution must be withheld for tax purposes.

With $100,000 in an IRA, Bob now elects to use rule 72(t). This provides Bob a monthly or annual payment of approximately $9,000/year. This $9,000 is taxable to Bob as ordinary income, but is not subject to the 10% penalty. He now takes the $9,000/year and puts it into a variable life insurance policy.

This raises a critical question: Why not leave the money in the IRA and let it grow on a tax-deferred basis? The problem lies with how large the IRA will grow, and how we can get it out. Say Bob left the money for 25 years. If current market rates continue, it would double every 6.5 years. That $100,000 would double almost four times to a nest egg of $1,500,000. When Bob finally withdrew the money, that money would be taxable as ordinary income. If he took out $80,000/year, that makes his social security taxable as well. (According to 1999 tax law, if the income is over $32,500 for married couples filing together, then Social Security is taxable.) This is a double loss.

Now let's say Bob only spend $80,000/year and passed away with an IRA balance of $800,000. Very likely, his heirs would receive only a small portion of this money after being taxed twice. First, income tax may be due and payable at that time on the entire amount. Also, estate taxes will be due on the money at that time. In the end, as much as 60% to 75% of that $800,000 will disappear to taxes. (And remember that they taxed his social security benefits getting here!)

So, Bob decided to put his $9,000/year into a plan that allowed him to get the money out tax-free. This is key, because most of the money he ended with was interest. If we had put $2000 into an IRA that invested in a S&P 500 mutual fund twenty years ago, today the fund would be worth an incredible $27,300! That shows the power of compounding interest.

A word of caution is in order here. IRS rule 72(t) has important restrictions you must be aware of. The actual rules consist of three pages of fine print, but the most important restriction deals with continuing the withdrawals. Once you start extracting money, you must take that amount every year until age 59.5, or suffer tax penalties on all the moneys thus far withdrawn.

VARIABLE LIFE INSURANCE

Instead of letting the money sit (or spending it), Bob set up a variable life policy and invested the $9,000/year. Here his interest grows tax-deferred. When he takes it out, it can be treated as a tax-free loan. He could use a Roth IRA instead of the Variable Life, but he could only deposit $2000/year, $4,000 if he was married. (This assumes Bob's annual income is less than $150,000 as well.) With this limitation, the Roth IRA will not meet Bob's needs.

Instead, Bob uses a Variable Life Insurance Policy with the death benefit set as low as possible. If he sets the death benefit far above the IRS's minimum amount, needless dollars would be lost paying for the cost of insurance. Thus, setting the low death benefit is a very important first step.

MAJOR ERROR: Making the death benefit in the Variable Life Policy higher than necessary. This will eat up valuable money paying for insurance. These charges are called Cost of Insurance (COI) fees.

Before using this strategy, Bob analyzed his options. The numbers for the two options he examined are detailed in the comparison on the next page.

Obviously, a client can benefit with tax-free income. This is very exciting, and the payout numbers stand on their own. In addition, the distributions from Variable Life do not count toward our $32,500 Social Security maximum! Thus, we may now receive our Social Security tax-free.

What is Variable Life? How does it work? You must understand it to use this strategy well. First, it resembles Whole Life and Universal Life with its expenses and fees. The main difference lies in the past returns of the investment accounts. If you look at recent 5, 10 and 20 year return on investments for Whole Life and Universal Life, you would find that they are slightly higher than the comparable returns for Certificates of Deposits (CDs). Since there is no direct correlation between them, we have to conclude that Whole Life and Universal Life are simply not good investments. Universal Life could become attractive if interest rates soared and the CD rates went up again, but with the current market, this is not a vehicle to use for an investment.

COMPARISON

Assume a $30,000 Deposit Each Year for 10 and 20 years
based on an 11% Annual Rate of Return

Option A: Deposit into the JanusFund for 10 to 20 Years. Tax Rate 35.75%. Withdrawals at Retirement and net income are included. The numbers are from a calculation.

Option B: Deposit into the Janus Fund inside a Variable Plan for 10 and 20 years. No taxes taken into account. The numbers are from an illustration.

ACCOUNT VALUES

10 YEARS	$501,660
20 YEARS	$1,926,084

10 YEARS	$466,808
20 YEARS	$1,623,666

The net income after 10 years would be $4,598/month, but after taxes are paid, the actual receipts is $2,954/month for the rest of your life. For 20 years, the net income would be $17,655 each month, before taxes are paid. The actual receipts are $11,343/month for life.

The assumptions made are for age 35, non- tobacco user, in excellent health, with minimum death benefits. After 10 years, the individual can receive $4,279/month for life. After 20 years, they can receive $14,883/month for life.

You need to know how to pick a variable life policy, and the key concerns when evaluating the policy. A Variable Life Policy is very complicated. There are limits on minimum and maximum contributions. The terminology seems designed to confuse, and page after page of tables further muddy the waters. To really determine the value of a contract, keep one thing in mind – dollars in compared to dollars out. In the above example, our internal rate of return exceeds 8% on our dollars, tax-free. In addition to the investment value, also remember that the policy provides a death benefit as well. This makes the analysis weigh in even more in favor of Variable Life or Variable Universal Life.

In many state, the law protects the money in this program from creditors. This protects your valuable asset in the event of bankruptcy, and is one more added benefit. Now, add in the fact that your life insurance was paid for (ie, the COI fees) with tax-free dollars. This differs from term insurance, which is paid with after tax dollars. This is another great advantage of this program.

To find out if a given policy will work well for you, ask the offering company for a comparison that shows dollars in versus dollars out. When you get this illustration, look at the value of the policy at years 1, 5, 10 and 20. Use a financial calculator to determine the internal rate of return over 10, 15 and 20 year periods.

If the values are high enough, ask one more question: Has this company typically paid more or less than the illustrated values? Many companies provide a very good illustration, but never meet the numbers they tout. This may result if they increase their cost to boost their profits. Other companies use conservative projections and have traditionally paid more than they have illustrated. At my firm we have three companies that fall in the latter category and we use those. If the company can not prove that they have historically paid the 'expected' returns, then their product is of no value to us.

MAJOR ERROR: Purchasing your variable life from a company who shows projections that are not reasonable or that they have not achieved in the past.

MINOR ERROR: Buying policies with extra riders. For each 'feature' you add to the policy, the insurance company adds costs, which comes out of your returns.

When deciding on a policy, pay careful attention to the value in year one. If there is a large up front cost, it will take a long time for your money to grow back. For example, let's say you started the policy with $30,000, and the value of the account is only $15,000 (based on current charges) after year one. This product will not work! It will take too long to make up the approximately $18,000 eaten up in first year charges. (The $18,000 is $15,000 of front-end charges plus $3,000 of interest.) In the same example, if the value is $27,000 in year one, then you have a good policy. First year costs of $6,000 ($3,000 each of up front costs and estimated interest) are very reasonable. This program will behave more like an investment and produce the outstanding results you need.

Beware of problems that are usually discovered after the policy is purchased. First, the program does not allow free access to the entire cash value at any given time. If you withdraw all the funds, you will face taxes due on the gain. So, if you have deposited $100,000 and the policy is currently worth $300,000, you should leave at least $15,000 in the program to keep the policy from lapsing. If the policy does lapse, prepare yourself for a huge tax bill (on $200,000 in this case). The best approach is to draw only interest from the funds, leaving the investment intact. If you did, however, need a large sum of money after the 10th year, you would need to adjust the face (death benefit) to the lowest possible amount and leave 5% in the plan to keep it in force.

Second, be wary of how much it costs you to withdraw your funds. Since the money will be taken as a loan that will never be repaid, you want the cost of the loan to be very low. This is of high importance.

Most companies charge a loan fee of around 1-2%. With compounding every year, this load fee will quickly eat away at your funds. You must try to find a policy that has a 'wash' loan, one with no fee to take a loan – the crediting rate is the same as the rate charged for the loan. Of the 2400 companies I have looked at, only twelve offered a wash loan. Two great companies that do (as of late 1999) are ITT Hartford and Jefferson Pilot.

When you purchase the policy, avoid any riders or other features. They cost money and deduct from the cash value build up. One notable exception may be a disability rider, which pays your premium if you get sick or hurt and cannot work. To determine if you want this rider, ask if it pays for the cost of insurance or for the entire amount you put into the policy. Of course, you prefer the latter since you would be putting large dollars in the policy over and above the cost of the insurance. After determining the rider's cost, you must decide whether the rider makes sense for you.

You must next consider which mutual funds to pick inside of the Variable Life contract. Remember that Variable Life only works for you if you invest for at least ten years. If your timeline is much shorter, or have a limited amount of money to work with, considering skipping the insurance in favor of investing directly in regular mutual funds.

There are five kinds of risk. You are punished for taking the first four, and rewarded for the fifth:
1. Single investment risk – putting all your money in one investment. If it tanks, you've lost your stake.
2. Single sector risk – investing solely in one industry. If you chose the automotive industry, and the government issued stringent emission requirements, chances are all your holdings would drop.
3. Interest rate risk – investing heavily in bonds. When interest rates rise, bond principals fall.

4. Purchasing power risk – fields including CDs, money market funds, and government securities. If your investments do not keep up with the rate of inflation, your real wealth decreases while your paper amount increases.
5. Stock market risk. Once again, you can not eliminate risk, but taken as a whole stocks have always risen over any many-year window looked at. The more widely diversified your holdings are, the better the chance you have to see substantial gains. Over any twenty-year period, there is a 99.6 % chance that stocks will out-perform the inflation and tax rate.

To achieve the best performance over the long run, pick the funds that are the most volatile (aggressive) and have a superior track record. Each company will have different sub accounts (also called separate accounts), but you want to pick the ones that have done better than the S&P 500 over the last 3, 5, and 10 years. You might look at technology and small cap stocks as well because of their volatility. One excellent portfolio might look like this:

> 33% Small Cap Index
> 34% S&P 500 Fund
> 33% Technology Sector Fund

Beware that sometimes your investment can drop in value. (This often happens during times of uncertainty, such as war, depression, recession, or when taxes and inflation are both high.) While this seems like bad news, it actually presents you with an opportunity. When stocks drop, you can buy shares at a discount.

Adding to your policy each year will result in 'dollar cost averaging'. (This means that you and/or your client add to the account each year on a consistent time interval basis.) Through dollar cost averaging, you will see some outstanding benefits from this method, related to buying when the market is down. However, your best results come when you put your money in the best funds. I recommend that you *not* put funds into bonds, money markets or any fixed accounts like GIC accounts, which pay a low rate of return.

INCOME TAX BENEFITS OF LIFE INSURANCE

Beneficiary income. This total death benefit consists of the amount of the policy-owner's equity accumulated within the contract and the earnings on that equity over the years, as well as the net amount at risk (the amount the insurance company would contribute if you died before fully funding the policy).

Inside build-up. The annual increases in value and the accumulated increases in value, whether through interest or investment appreciation, are not taxed when earned, and will escape taxation entirely provided they are eventually delivered as a death benefit. Transactions among the mutual funds within the policy are also not subject to current taxation.

Policy "cost basis". This includes funds spent on expenses and mortality cost within a policy, making such expenditures tax-free whether a policy terminates as a death benefit or otherwise.

Policy loan. With the significant exception (as of June 20, 1988) of modified endowment policies that exceed the seven-pay threshold (more on this later), you can generally access policy values via policy loans, collateralizations, or withdrawals without incurring taxes or penalties. Note the difference between life insurance (no 10% penalty on withdrawals before age 59½) and annuities (which generally do not allow loans).

DEATH BENEFITS – TAX-FREE

The primary benefit of life insurance is that, for small contributions over the years, your beneficiary will receive a large payoff when you subsequently die. This benefits not only you and your beneficiaries, but all of us too. Your heirs do not depend on us (i.e., society) through welfare.

For this reason, death benefits of life insurance policies have been exempted from income tax. It doesn't matter whether the death benefit comes from net amount at risk, the policy-owner's investment in the contract, or positive investment results. It is *all* tax-free under Section 101 of the Internal Revenue Code. This, the first income-tax benefit of life insurance, is enjoyed by all life insurance policyholders.

However, you can mismanage your policy in such ways that result in taxes. For instance, if you sell your death benefit to obtain cash (known as *viaticals,* a growing business among AIDS sufferers who need money for medical bills), the sale will be fully taxed. Don't make any such moves without considering them carefully with your tax advisor.

CURRENT EARNINGS AND GAINS NOT CURRENTLY TAXED

The second advantage of life insurance is that while the policy is in force, all interest and dividends earned and capital gains in the policy are not subject to current income tax. You can even take gains from a very profitable policy fund and move them to another fund within the contract, without running afoul of taxes and (often) transaction costs. Taxes are deferred until you withdraw the gains. All investment life insurance policies provide for tax-deferral on this inside build up and the possibility of total tax-exemption on investment returns if the proceeds are disbursed as death benefits.

TAX BASIS INCLUDES PAYMENTS FOR LIFE INSURANCE EXPENSES

The third income-tax benefit of life insurance, containing investment capital, is the amount of money you recover, tax-free, when you surrender your policy and have a gain. Your tax basis includes all the life insurance costs the policy has incurred during the time the policy has been in force. In this situation, the costs increase your basis and thus are recovered tax-free. For example, if you paid premiums of $10,000/year for twenty years and the insurance costs ran another $1000 yearly, your cost basis would be $220,000, which includes the cost of the insurance. If you surrendered the policy for $400,000, your gain would be $180,000.

TAX-FREE USE OF UNTAXED EARNINGS AND GAINS

The fourth income-tax benefit is that you can use the values accumulated within the life insurance policy while it is in force, and still 1) withdraw, 2) borrow against them, or 3) pledge the policy as collateral for a loan (e.g., borrow from a bank). If you withdraw an amount exceeding the amount you've invested, the amount withdrawn above your cost is subject to ordinary income tax. Don't do it! If you need additional funds, take a loan against the policy or use the policy as collateral to get at those funds while avoiding taxes. Prior to June 20, 1988, you could do this on almost any policy without paying income tax on the accumulated gain within the contract. However, as of that date, Uncle Sam limited the amount you could invest in a policy.

MODIFIED ENDOWMENT INSURANCE-TAMRA 88

Single-premium life policies are the most investment-oriented. In effect, they become maximum-funded policies with the first and only premium. Prior to June 21, 1988, they combined (1) high returns (because of relatively high interest rates available at that time) with (2) a deferral (no tax on those returns), and (3) the ability to access those returns without incurring taxes.

In 1988 Congress decided this was too lucrative for us taxpayers – a tax shelter for John Q. Public. As a result, in November congress passed the Technical and Miscellaneous Revenue Act (TAMRA) of 1988. This new law defined *modified endowment policies*, a new class of life insurance policies that included single-premium life policies.

The new law removed tax-free accessibility to the cash in the policies. Any policy issued after June 20, 1988, classified as a modified endowment policy contract (MEC), cannot provide the policy-owner rights to withdraw from, borrow from, or collateralize the money within the policy without incurring immediate taxation on policy gains. Indeed, if you are under 59½, not only do income taxes become due on the amount of the gain you access, but you also must pay a 10% penalty on the amount included in gross income as a result of the transaction. You may escape this penalty only if you withdraw the funds as a result of disability or over a period related to the policy-owner's lifetime (annuitized).

HOW TO AVOID MODIFIED ENDOWMENT STATUS

For investment purposes you, as the policy-owner, want all four income tax benefits. In particular, you want the ability to withdraw up to the basis or loans on your policy without exposing it to ordinary income tax or penalties. To accomplish this with a policy issued after June 20, 1988, you may invest no more during the first seven years than the amount determined by the government-mandated test called the *seven-pay test*. This test limits the amount you can invest in your policy in the first seven years of its existence.

For example, if the insurance company offering you a policy informs you (*and it should*) that the seven-pay test allows no more $1,000 per policy year, you could put up to, but no more than, $1,000 into the policy in the first year. You could put in, but no more than, a total of $2,000 by the end of the second year. For the first seven policy years, the cumulative maximum you could contribute would be

$7,000. At that point, your policy would have completed the testing period, and would not be a modified endowment contract. Now you could take loans or withdrawals up to basis without worrying about taxes.

In addition, the amount of the contributions to your policy is controlled by other provisions of the Internal Revenue Code (IRC), Section 7702. Indeed, you will often find these more restrictive in the fifth through seventh policy years, than the seven-pay test restrictions. You may not be able to contribute even up to the seven-pay test limits. Your insurance company should inform you if your contributions have exceeded either those allowed by IRC, Section 7702 or the seven-pay test limits and refund any excess to you. Most insurance companies offer tracking assistance. Find out how yours does it.

TARGET PREMIUM

You will find target premium referred to over and over again as you examine sales loads and surrender charges. It is determined when your policy is issued. Your age, sex, whether you smoke, and your policy face amount all influence this figure. Target premium for variable life is generally around 75% of a typical whole-life annual premium. The insurance company will give you this all-important number.

Once determined, the target premium then defines the level on which commissions for the selling insurance agent are based. Normally, the commission payable on these policies is about 50% of the target premium plus 4% of payments in excess of the target premium. The agent also earns commissions if the policyholder requests an increase in the face amount of the policy. Upon continued investment into your policy for years two through ten, renewal commissions average 4% of premium paid. After ten years, the rate drops to 2%. The 2% is a transferable service fee payable to the agent servicing the policy-owner and is currently applicable only to new money being paid into the contract. These commissions are paid out of the expenses you pay to the insurance company. (Note that what the insurance company deducts from your policy payments does not cover their expenses. It advances the agent's payments and amortizes them out of what the company earns in future years.)

There has been, and continues to be, pressure to reduce sales commissions. Many people feel that moving from high first-year and low renewal commissions toward a more level commission and charge, based upon assets under management, would better serve salespeople, the insurance company, and you. With these policies, the help of a knowledgeable agent to manage policy profitably can be invaluable. You want continued long-term interest in you and your contract. The commission system of today, though, does not encourage that. The agents can't spend time managing your money if they are not paid to do so.

ADMINISTRATION FEES

First-year administration fees typically exceed ongoing administration fees. The higher fee in year one covers the costs of setting up the policy and costs incurred in determining if you are healthy, wealthy, and cautious enough to buy a policy. The average first-year cost is between $300 and $400, with a high of $600 to $700.

Range of Administration Fees

Low	Average	High
$200	$300 - $400	$700

ON-GOING MONTHLY ADMINISTRATION FEE

This fee enables the insurance company to provide continuous services such as mailing confirmation notices, preparing periodic reports, providing telephone reporting, the prospectus and annual reports. It can run $4 to $15 a month, with $5 to $7 being typical. The company will tell you what they charge, and the maximum it can charge by contract.

Continuing Administration Fees

Low	Average	High
$4/mo	$5-$7/mo	$8-$15/mo

FEES FOR SERVICES
Moving Your Investments Within Your Policy

Your universal variable policy gives you the right to move your existing investment among the mutual funds within your policy, but may limit the number of moves you may make per year and/or charge for the moves. You'd like to have the freedom to move funds as often as possible at the least cost. Most companies make no charge for four moves per year, and charge up to $25 per move after that.

MOVES PER YEAR

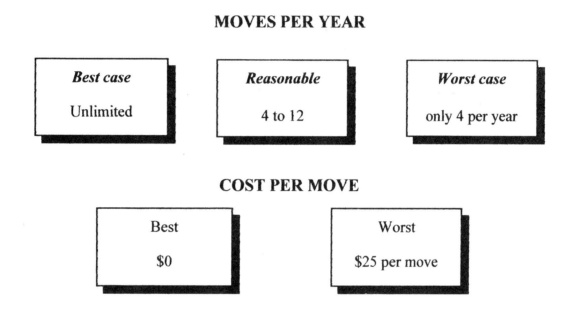

Best case	*Reasonable*	*Worst case*
Unlimited	4 to 12	only 4 per year

COST PER MOVE

Best	Worst
$0	$25 per move

POLICY LOANS AND WITHDRAWALS

Pay close attention to the provisions relating to policy loans and withdrawals. They tell you how to get your money out of the policy without terminating it. (You can expect to be charged $25 to process a withdrawal.) These figures determine the liquidity of your universal variable life investment. When you ask for information about loans and withdrawals, the insurance company will give it to you in terms of surrender value. This is the cash sum you receive if you cash out the policy, which equals the accumulation value less the surrender charge.

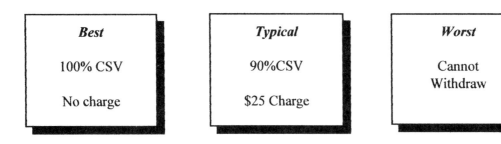

Best	Typical	Worst
100% CSV	90%CSV	Cannot Withdraw
No charge	$25 Charge	

WHAT IS "SPREAD"?

People do get confused about policy loans. They think they are taking money out of their policies, but they aren't. Actually, they are borrowing from the insurance company, using their policies as perfect collateral. If you don't pay off your loan, eventually the insurance company will take the money from your policy or the death benefit.

Policy Loans

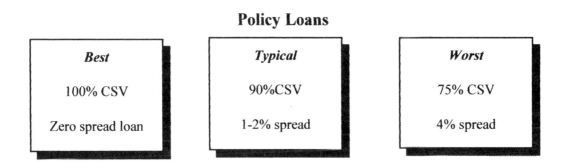

Best	Typical	Worst
100% CSV	90%CSV	75% CSV
Zero spread loan	1-2% spread	4% spread

When you borrow X dollars, the company takes X dollars from your policy and moves it into the loan guarantee fund. This fund then earns interest for you. Thus, you are paying interest to the company for money you borrowed, and the company is paying you interest on the amount in the loan guarantee fund. The difference between the two is called the "spread."

Typically the interest rate on the loan guarantee runs 2% less than your loan rate. At worst, you could be paying the company up to 4% in excess of what they are paying you. At best the company could charge a zero spread, which means the interest rate you pay and you get are the same. This *wash loan* is the type of loan you want to get.

Let us look at a statement (next page) of a person who actually purchased a Variable Life policy. Notice that this person purchased the policy in May 1993 and has had it for 3 years. These are actual numbers. The person had put in

Policy Owner: John Doe
                 123 Easy Str
                 Aurora, CO 80015

Annual Policy Statement
Individual Flexible Premium
Variable Life Insurance
Period: May 15, 1995 – May 14, 1996

Policy No: xxxxxxx

POLICY SPECIFICATIONS

Insured:	Confidential	Issue Date:	May 15, 1993
Date of Statement:	May 14, 1996	Maturity Date:	May 15, 2046
Sex:	Male	Issue State:	Colorado
Tax ID Number:	456-78-2000	State of Residence:	Colorado
Initial Specified Amount:	$1,200,000	Policy Status:	Active

SUMMARY OF INSURANCE BENEFITS
As of May 14, 1996

ANNUAL ACCOUNT SUMMARY
As of May 14,1996

Death Benefit Option 1	$1,200,000.00	Beginning Accumulation Value	$	76,811.31
Accumulation Value	$ 102,401.99	Gross Payments	$	0.00
Surrender Charge	-$ 5,000.40	Annual Cost of Insurance	- $	3,390.29
Cash Value	$ 97,401.59	Annual Expense Charges	- $	72.00
Surrender Value	$ 97,401.59	Gain/Loss	$	29,052.97
		Ending Accumulation Value		$102,401.99

POLICY VALUES

	Beginning Value May 15, 1995	Ending Value May 14, 1996	Projected Value May 14, 1997
Death Benefit	$1,200,000.00	$1,200,000.00	$1,200,000.00
Accumulation Value	$ 76,811.31	$ 102,401.99	$ 125,651.24
Surrender Charge	-$ 5,000.40	-$ 5,000.40	-$ 5,000.40
Cash Value	$ 71,810.91	$ 97,409.59	$ 120,650.84
Surrender Value	$ 71.810.91	$ 97,401.59	$ 120,650.84

To comply with various state requirements, values projected one year in advance assume that (1) planned periodic premiums are paid as scheduled; (2) guaranteed cost of insurance is deducted; (3) the charge for state premium taxes, investment advisory fee, expenses, and mortality and expenses risk charges remain at their present rates, and (4) the hypothetical gross rate of return is equal to zero. Death benefit: in accordance with the investment experience of Separate Account A, the cash values and the variable death benefit may increase or decrease. The death benefit is the amount less the loan amount and the loan interest due, payable to the beneficiary under the policy upon death of the insured.
Option 1: The death benefit usually will remain level throughout the life of the policy

Produced May 16,1996

$20,000/year for three years and skipped the fourth year to buy a boat. This Annual Policy Summary is for the fourth year, which is May 1995 to May 1996.

The person was a healthy 41-year-old non-smoker. He wanted to set up a plan that would add the interest from his investments for fifteen years. The sub account used was the Janus Twenty fund. Notice the fees and charges for $1,200,000 of death benefit are $3,390 for the year of this statement. Since the $3,390 is paid from earnings, this insurance was purchased with tax-free money.

It is important to note that the minimum insurance was $595,000 for this person. He chose the $1,200,000 because he had three children and needed the death benefit to protect his family. His cost of insurance was double of what the typical person would pay. Did you see that the policy paid $29,052.97 in interest during this period? This is a great example of putting your money to work!

REBALANCING

Rebalancing offers an opportunity to add to your return. In a variable life policy you may exercise the option to rebalance your money. To do this means to take the sub accounts and even them up at the end of the year.

Let's say you have three accounts as we suggested above, and the technology paid 40% return, the index paid 10%, and the small cap fund had a negative 20% return. Your funds are now out of balance, since the technology fund has much more money than the small cap fund. To rebalance, you must move money from the technology to the small cap fund.

This process guarantees that you sell high and buy low. Following this rule generally promises the best return over the long haul. Notice the attached example where a person put $1000 each into five well-known funds. If left alone for ten years, the funds would have grown to $28,819.23 – an 19.14% average annual gain. However, if they were rebalanced, the same five funds would grow to $30,179.05 – an even better deal at 19.69%.

The mantra for success in the stock market is obvious: "Buy low, sell high." However, human nature tends to ignore that. If you've got a winner, why not stick with it? What gains are you giving up by selling too soon? And why move your funds to an under-performer?

As you can see from the above example, rebalancing forces you to show good investor behavior and buy low/sell high. Did you see how often a fund that does well one year, follows that with a shockingly poor year? For example, the Invesco Strategic Health Science fund paid 91.8% in 1991, and then returned a negative 13.4% and 8.4%, respectively, in 1992 and 1993. In this situation it is wise to take our profits and run to a new investment.

FUND NAME	Return as a % Ending Dec. 31st of each year									
	86	87	88	89	90	91	92	93	94	95
FIDELITY Equity Growth	14.5	(.57)	15.6	44.8	6.9	64.7	9.9	14.8	(0.9)	39.1
ALLIANCE	12.0	19.2	0.6	6.0	(3.8)	54.2	15.5	21.6	28.5	45.8
INVESCO Strat Hlth Sci	29.4	7.1	16.0	59.5	25.8	91.8	(13.4)	(8.4)	0.9	58.8
T ROWE PRICE International	61.3	8.0	17.9	23.7	(8.9)	15.9	(3.5)	40.1	(0.8)	16.8
PUTNAM Voyager	20.1	10.8	11.9	34.8	(2.8)	50.3	9.7	18.4	0.4	40.2
average value	1275	1386	1562	2088	2180	3454	3458	3908	4076	5764
rebalanced value	1275	1388	1560	2087	2159	3354	3476	4078	4307	6036

ANOTHER BENEFIT OF VARIABLE LIFE

The growing size of mutual funds has become an area of great concern. In many cases, fund managers can no longer purchase exactly what they want. Too often, fund managers are limited to buying fewer stocks than they wish to buy. For example, say that a fund manager wants to put 5% of his fund into IBM. He may find that the most he can purchase amounts to 1.3% of his fund, since otherwise his holdings will violate the maximum holding rules.

It's different with variable life. The insurance sub-accounts act differently than mutual funds even though they look, smell, and act the same. Think of a sub-account as merely a copy of a mutual fund, without the holding restrictions. A sub-account is created by the mutual fund family, and uses the same fund manager. He will effect the same buying and selling as the mutual fund, but the small fund (because of its size) will not have the same constraints as the large fund. It can often have more money in the places the fund manager desires, and less in his second or third choice.

In exhibit 3, the three year return for the Janus Mercury fund is given at 23.01% and the sub-account called the Pacific Select Growth LT is given at 24.62%. This large difference arises due to the freedom the manager has working with the sub-account.

Exhibit 3

Alternative Distribution Group   FAX

To: _____Alan Gay_____

Company: _____

Phone Number: ___306 - 6377_____

Fax Number: _____306 - 9375_____

Number of Pages including cover sheet: ____1_____

Phone Number: ____303-336-7869_____

Date: ____12-3-97_____

Comments: _____Performance as of September 30, 1997_____

	1 month	3 year
PACIFIC SELECT GROWTH LT* _____	6.17	24.62____
JANUS MERCURY _____	5.85	23.01____

* Before expenses

Fillmore Place	Ptarmigan	Galleria
100 Fillmore Street	3773 Cherry Creek North Dr	720 South Colorado Boulevard
Denver, CO 80206	Denver, CO 80209	Denver, CO 80222

J A N U S   F U N D S

This very important benefit may grow even more crucial in the next century. I predict that margins for most funds will grow larger, and the sub-accounts will greatly outperform their more unwieldy counterparts. As seen in the above example, some sub-accounts already beat the fund they copy. Those return margins could quickly grow even more substantial.

In summary, variable life offers a tremendous advantage in owning sub-accounts, or small copies of the actual mutual funds. These sub-accounts will have restrictions due to their size, thus offering greater potential returns than the actual funds.

The purpose of this chapter was to show you how to change your money from taxable to tax-free. This concept ranks as one of the most important you can learn. To do this for your family or a client puts them miles ahead at retirement. I hope you can adapt to the method and products used to make this work. If you have an open mind, this could send their earnings soaring.

Do not be concerned if some people downplay this concept. For some reason, using variable insurance invokes a great deal of emotion. It could be due, partially, to the old whole life contracts that we purchased as investments, which did not work out well as other investments. You must have an open mind to achieve tax-free money at retirement.

CHAPTER 3

THE FIVE AREAS OF AN EXTRAORDINARY LIFE

Have you ever had a great success, but still felt like something was missing?

Maybe your life wasn't 'in balance'.

I'm sure you've heard that "money can't buy happiness," or "If you don't have your health, you don't have anything." This hints at the complexity of life, that there are several pieces to the 'puzzle' of a great life. Many sages, when talking about getting the most from life, refer to having a 'balanced life'.

Growing up, I remember people giving me advice: "Don't forget about a balanced life Al." "Take time for your spiritual life." "That poor person? His life is out of balance." This notion of 'balance', though, no one ever defined for me. Twenty-four years of college and advanced studies didn't address it, and I still see people struggle with it.

Certainly, to be an interesting person, you need to experience growth in more than just one area. To truly like ourselves and be admired by others, we need to be well-rounded. We can only achieve this by continually growing.

Though none of the areas of life can stand alone, and all influence each other, they can be summarized in the following categories:
- Business and financial success
- Spiritual growth
- Physical health
- Joy, Happiness and Inner Peace
- Friendships

Note that these are in no special order. Each will have different values to different people at different times. However, every area is important, and no one should completely neglect an area if they hope to attain a truly 'balanced life'.

The most delightful and satisfied people I have ever met have at least some success in all of these areas. On the other hand, many unhappy people have been successful in only one or none of these areas. Every morning when they look in the mirror they admit, "I am sad because I am not good at life".

Anyone can achieve success in any one area of life. For an example, take the spiritual area. To be instantly successful, you could attend church every Sunday morning and again on Wednesday night. On Monday and Tuesday stay home all day, reading the bible and spiritual writings. On Thursday spend the entire day in prayer. On Friday and Saturday, discuss spiritual matters the entire day with others more enlightened than you. After one year, you will achieve great spiritual growth!

But, does this spiritual growth come at a price you could afford? What would it cost to neglect the other four areas of your life? Lost friendships? Money worries? To be truly successful, you must find a way to nurture all five areas of your life and improve in each area, every year.

I feel you will have no better chance to grow in all five areas each year than in the financial service profession. Why? Because you will improve financially each year, giving you the opportunity and time to work on the other areas. You can become one of the rare people to make progress toward a balanced life. Oh baby! Are these people interesting to talk to around the dinner table.

In this chapter we will focus on constant, continual improvement in all five areas, with a particular emphasis on financial. At this time we'll assume that the financial will be your foundation. You can then use this as leverage in the other areas of your life.

CRITICAL ERROR: Do not work exclusively in one area on a long-term basis at the expense of the other areas. The key is to make constant continual progress in each area. At times, of course, you must concentrate in one area exclusively, but make sure to limit these periods. Progress in only one area provides little fulfillment, and thus has little benefit.

This book assumes that you have not yet made significant progress in any of the five areas. If you already have a beautiful family and lots of friends that love you, or if you enjoy good health and have made great strides financially, or in your spiritual life, congratulations! You are starting at a tremendous advantage. In fact, you are light years ahead of the crowd.

Let us look carefully at each area. At the end, decide in which area you want to improve first.

BUSINESS AND FINANCIAL

Do not underestimate the importance of money! In our society, it is of key importance. We trade money for things like college education, homes and cars. I remember trading a few dollars for airline tickets so my parents' best friends could help celebrate my parents' 50th wedding anniversary. Those friends made their anniversary special just by being there.

Money provides options and lets you make immediate impacts on the other areas. In fact, I have seen individuals with great financial success hire people to guide them to success in the other areas.

Your path in life will require a conscious decision of how much and when to improve each area of your life. As soon as you have achieved the success that you desire in the financial arena, move quickly into the others. For now, though, let us look at gaining success in the financial area. If you follow a few suggestions, you will have an excellent chance to succeed.

Have you ever noticed people who really love their work? Their enthusiasm infects those around them. They brim with energy, and spread smiles at the office. At times it seems like they're (*gasp*) having <u>fun</u>!

Their key? They work *ex animo* – from the heart. They do what they love, and money is not their prime motivation. For them, the reward comes from accomplishing a task they care about. People like this, you could say, never work a day in their life – because their work is their play. Ronald Reagan once said, "I have heard a little hard work never hurt anyone, but I do not want to take any chances." Mr. Reagan obviously found a profession he could work *ex animo*.

A person who can find such a career has great potential. He can bring greater focus and energy to what he or she does, giving them an advantage in the workplace. If someone of average intelligence and motivation can work *ex animo*, they will typically see a 10% or greater increase in pay each year.

Remember in the movie *Lion King*, where Timon and the warthog had no cares? They called in "Hakuna Matata", a Swahili phrase meaning "no worries (problems) for the rest of your days." If you can work *ex animo*, you may feel the same. Thus, I call working in your area of special expertise "operating in your Hakuna Matata."

It is sad to me that very few people take the time to find their special area of expertise. Some people work in a job they do not enjoy, slaving away their best years for money. They trade their freedom for a paycheck.

Other people excel at their work, but it does not excite them. They coast through their days, but the golden ring of success stays just out of reach. There is no doubt that finding your Hakuna Matata is the key to success.

Are you working in that special area? If not, take time to find it. In solitude, answer the following questions. Brainstorm! Do not judge your answers. Put down everything that comes to mind for each question. (It may help to listen to soft, relaxing music as you think these things over.)

Question 1: If I could not fail, what would I do for a career?

Question 2: If I had unlimited money and did not need to work, what would I do?

Question 3: If I had only two years to live (assume you would have perfect health), what work would I do during that two years?

Once you have compiled your responses, look for any answers that are repeated. These indicate high levels of interest on your part. Could you move toward a career in one of these areas? It could change your life!

For an exercise, let's look at some sample answers and what they might mean.

To **Question 1,** an imaginary tester answered:
1. Open a construction company with up to a dozen employees.
2. Create a ministry similar in size to Focus on the Family for single parents.
3. Own a missionary support company and travel throughout the world to assist the 100 or so missionaries that this organization supports.
4. Create a college or university that offers an alternative education.

The answers to **Question 2** included:
1. Open a combined restaurant/spiritual bookstore in the nicest part of town.
2. See answer (3) above.
3. Travel throughout the world with my bride and family, seeing all parts and cultures of this great world.
4. Give millions of dollars to charities that work to reverse the current increase in violence in North America.

Questions 3 was answered thus:

1. I would spend time with my family and support them in what they considered important.
2. Same as (3) above.
3. I would play a part in the lives of those I care for, and show genuine appreciation and love for them.
4. I would create a positive radio station, which played upbeat music with a good message. The radio station would also have humor and positive news about people who make a difference with their life.

With these answers you should see exactly where your interest lies. The book Think and Grow Rich states that you can have anything which you can conceive. The actual quote is, "There is nothing capricious in nature." I would go so far as to say that if you do not have these things in your life, then your life is less than it could have been. I can think of nothing worse than knowing you could have created these things and had a fulfilled life, and yet you missed it.

After deciding which of these things you are most excited and passionate about, work on it every day. Spend at least 10 minutes (or more – aim for an hour!) working on it, and make some progress daily.

If you take nothing else from this book, please take this advice. Find what you are passionate about. Go after it! I promise you will never regret it. A life of passion is the best kind of life.

If after doing this, you are still not clear on where your Hakuna Matata lies, take a personality test. This test gives you suggestions of careers which match your personality. I took one, and it surprised me by listing several options I had not considered as possibilities. This test may give you additional insights beyond weighing careers that you currently know about.

Several tests will point you to those occupations you might like and those you should avoid. In our office we use the KOLBE test. This test provides you a list of twenty careers to consider and twenty to avoid. If you'd like the phone number for the KOLBE Corporation, you may contact our office.

Following are some excellent questions that may help bring your current situation into focus. In solitude, ask these questions and dig deep into yourself for answers. Ask these questions every six months. Write down three to five answers for each.

(If you've already accomplished the item asked, erase the question and move on. At age 38, I felt totally financially secure but my spouse did not. Thus, I ignored the second half of that question. If you have just effected a plan to multiply your income by ten but needed two years to complete it, take that off the list until your plan concludes. Then, return the question to the list.)

CRITICAL ERROR: Not working in your Hakuna Matata. It is absolutely key for a good life that you not only work in a career you excel at, but one that excites you as well. Since these things change, you must look at them at least every three months. This is key to your financial situation. We will talk more about this later, and even give it a name.

Questions:

1. What is great about my current financial situation?

2. What can I do right now to multiply my income by 10 times my current income?

3. How much do I need to make to allow me to reduce the hours I work and move my focus into other areas of my life?

4. What has to happen for my spouse to feel financially secure? How does this compare with what has to happen for you to feel financially secure?

5. Do I currently enjoy my work and am I excellent at what I do?

SPIRITUAL

This was the most exciting area on my path to discovery! On your journey, you will likely find your growth here to be the most fulfilling. I can think of nothing worse than going through life thinking that when our body stops functioning, everything ends. To believe we are alone and in no way connected to a loving force, or to each other, is profoundly sad! Today, we should ask ourselves, "What can we do to join our fellow man?" People could benefit by asking, "Do I want to be happy, or do I want to be right?"

Most people work out their spiritual beliefs just before they pass away (assuming they have time). It makes their transition from form to formless a very traumatic experience. What could have been a great celebration of a wonderful life is lost.

I had a friend I met in the Colorado National Guard. He was outspoken and very often harsh. He found it difficult to give grace or forgiveness, instead letting his punitive nature shine through. As far as I know, he had never dwelled on things spiritual. When I asked him about his beliefs, he replied, "I tend to look at God very much like my father: dysfunctional, unloving and judgmental."

How sad! To think that when you pass away, you will go live with someone like this. One day he found out that lymph and gland cancer had spread throughout his body. In the short two months before he passed away, he concentrated on finally growing in the spiritual area.

He learned to pray, and for the first time, found a connection between him and his creator. He finally said 'thank you' for the things he had experienced. In the end, he saw God and others – and life – differently, separating them from his experience with his father.

In my spiritual journey, I feel a special happiness and satisfaction having learned these special lessons. I found great solace during my spiritual journey through reading the Bible. For me to discover that the Bible is full of codes proved to me that it is, indeed, the word of God! How wonderful!

I capped my discovery by learning prayer, which allowed me to feel a closeness and connection with God and others in my life. I rank that as my greatest spiritual gift. You should learn to pray, using either intercessory or request prayers.

When you pray intercessory, you say, "Thy will be done." Introverts may find this the ultimate prayer, since it acknowledges God's wisdom and gives them the chance to look at the key areas in their life. An intercessory prayer could say, "With regard to Bill who is sick, Thy will be done; With regard to my test next week, Thy will be done; In my relationship with my wife and with matters I have forgotten to address, Thy will be done". God knows our needs and will meet them.

I call the other type of prayer 'request prayer'. Here we create a laundry list of things that concerned us. We might say, "Please help me get ____; please build up my immune system; please help me make an 'A' on my test Monday." This prayer works just as well as an intercessory.

At times we may not really know what to pray for. For example, if we pray to build up our immune system, we may get the disease of an overactive immune system. If we ask for an 'A' on the test, we may discover that it overqualified us for a career in the area we wanted. When I pray, I try to leave the situation open for the best possible result, and trust that God will give it to me.

Because prayer allows us to reach out and touch others in the next room, or on the other side of the planet, I predict this area will see great interest and growth in the near future. In fact, studies have already shown that prayer makes a tremendous difference in any career or profession. Those who pray for their clients and their relationships will make a difference in their lives and with their lives.

Find your own spiritual path. Know what you believe and why. As I look back, my spiritual journey was certainly my greatest discovery. How wonderful and exciting were the principals I learned. I remember the greatest lesson, that the "best part of me is not born so it does not die."

In my journey, only what I create in love will last. Everything that I created in love will shine after I go; everything else, no matter how great, will turn to dust.

After accepting Jesus Christ in my life as my personal savior, and developing my prayer life, I can actually sense his love and healing, and feel a unique and exciting freshness in my life. I feel great hope and optimism for my time in this world and in the next. Best of all, I always feel connected. I never feel lonely because of this Divine connection.

Make your spiritual journey a high priority! Then you can have this grace and completeness in your life.

CRITICAL ERROR: Failing to pursue your spiritual journey, because you have not found a religion, denomination, church or thinking that suits you. Your spiritual journey could be one of the most important and exciting areas in your life. Don't miss it! You may see your money disappear, you may lose your health, your friends may pass away before you, leaving you with only your spiritual beliefs. Your "spirit" and your spiritual foundation could be your solace and your foundation. It could be your sole source of mental peace. Never underestimate the importance of your spiritual journey.

Questions:

1. What am I most interested in, in my spiritual journey?

2. What is important enough in my life to pray for?

3. Am I most comfortable with intercessory prayer or request prayer?

4. What can I create out of love for my fellow man, that will last and make a difference in our lives?

5. What can I do, today, to join with the people in my life?

6. What am I most excited about in my spiritual journey?

7. Who might be my spiritual advisor?

8. What books and information might I read, that would provide me with the greatest spiritual growth?

9. What must happen for me to consider myself a great spiritual being?

PHYSICAL HEALTH

The physical area greatly interests and excites me. In 1999, I completed the Pikes Peak Marathon for the 16th consecutive year. This grueling race covers fourteen miles from Colorado Springs to Pikes Peak, and another fourteen miles back down. It took me nine hours, twenty-nine minutes, barely beating ten hours – at which time the course closed! In 1984, I completed my first Pikes Peak Marathon in 6:26. Each year after that it took a little longer to complete. Isn't aging a pain?

I pay close attention to my health. To perform at a high level, I can't be sick or sluggish. I know my health directly affects the length and quality of my life. A wise man, summarizing the importance of health, said, "What could be more disappointing than seeing success in your career, your relationships, and finally being satisfied with your life, only to find that, due to bad health, this will all be very short lived".

EXERCISE

Those who work out regularly have a secret: Exercise feels good!

Recently I read a wonderful health book. According to the book, if you have a healthy aerobic system, you have an excellent opportunity to surpass your life expectancy in good health (with a very high quality of life). You can create and maintain a healthy aerobic system with only fifteen minutes of aerobic activity, three times each week. Just think! Fifteen minutes of running, swimming, biking, spinning, playing tennis, squash, or racquetball, or practicing aerobics will do it. What do **you** like to do?

With this knowledge alone, you are well on your way to great health. But even more intriguing for me was how I felt when I increased my workouts from fifteen to forty-five minutes (still three times per week). I have noticed a complete difference in how I feel physically and emotionally. It was a remarkable change, almost as if I took medication. According to my personal trainer, the change is due to my body releasing endorphins. These body chemicals bring a feeling of comfort and euphoria. I feel more content, more relaxed, more alive and more at peace with the world. Somehow everything comes into perspective.

Being a very high strung person, this helps me calm down. Why didn't I know this before? For some reason, people don't bother writing about this – even though they have known it for many years. I find it astounding that you could get guaranteed good health, feel good and gain a sense of well-being with only forty-five minutes, three times each week.

This must be the most overlooked way to better your life. I only wonder, "Why don't more people do it?"

REDUCE STRESS

Do things ever fly out of control? Do you feel the muscles in your neck tensing? Is it impossible to get things going smoothly?

Stress is an insidious evil. It saps you of strength, keeps your mind out of focus, makes you snap at friends. It lowers your immune system, leaving you vulnerable to sickness. But it doesn't have to control you!

If you feel stress building, do this simple exercise: Take a long slow breath. Breathe in, hold your breath and then breathe out, taking five seconds for each step (fifteen seconds for in-hold-out cycle). After exhaling say to yourself, "I am relaxed and confident." Repeat all steps until you again have perspective. Try this when you are upset at someone and in danger of losing your temper!

SLEEP

You cannot have great health without getting enough sleep. While missing a little sleep will not kill you, it can affect how you feel and severely impair your judgement. I got into the habit of not getting enough sleep in the military. At Lackland Air Base in San Antonio, we rose at 4:30 a.m. and had a vigorous schedule until 8 p.m., when I fell into a level of sleep resembling a coma.

I noted the amount of work I accomplished on this schedule. After leaving the military, I tried to continue it. While I always accomplished a great deal of work, based on the sheer volume of tasks I completed, in hindsight I realize that much of the work was not of the highest quality. I could have gotten my sleep, and produced better results!

In a state of sleep deprivation, the average person is only 60-80% as effective as someone who has had 90% or more of the needed sleep. Consider this: you could have downtime of 20% of your week, and still accomplish the same amount. What could you accomplish with your career – or in other areas of your life – with that extra time?

What if you can't sleep? First try this exercise: Breathe as described above, in for five seconds, hold for five, exhale for five. As you exhale, tighten your muscles, beginning at the top or bottom and going through your entire body. Next, release it and do nothing but relax for five seconds. Continue this exercise until you begin to relax.

If this does not work, get out of bed and write down anything bothering you. Let's say you are concerned about your work. Maybe you made a mistake and need to admit that to a client. You might even lose the deal. Simply take a white sheet of paper and write down the worse thing that could happen. Somehow, this takes all the fear and concern out of the situation and putting everything suddenly back into perspective.

DIET

For me, diet ranks below exercise and sleep in priority. Maybe this results from my upbringing, where a relatively poor diet and my lack of attention to food did not seem to affect my health. Growing up in Georgia and Alabama, I became a fast friend to fried food. In addition to my grease consumption, I very much enjoy my potato chips and my excessive calories. For the past twenty years my caloric intake has stayed about 20% above what I actually needed.

I do not suggest, however, that diet is of no importance. Food keeps our bodies running, and can help us fend off disease. One great rule of thumb is, "**If it is not delicious, then do not eat it**"! Think how things would change if we did not eat food that only tasted mediocre to us. We would consume less and would feel better. This would improve the overall dining experience because, when we did eat, we would enjoy it more.

(The same law can be applied to finances as well. "If you do not love it, do not buy it." We should feel that we can not live without something before we purchase it. Most people who overspend, purchase things that are 'nice'. When they find things they truly need, or would really like to have, they find their money went to purchase things that were not extraordinary. I believe any purchase should speak to you and who you are before you consider owning it. You can also apply this same concept to the other areas. For example, "Only date a person you would be proud to marry; only work for the best company; only go to a church that you are proud of; and relating to this chapter, only eat it if it is delicious.")

In 1990 I had the distinct pleasure of visiting Japan for 2 weeks. The lessons I learned there greatly impacted my life. My colleagues and I worked with Hineaka Tinneca, a major in the Japanese military. He told me of the two major differences between the Japanese and the Americans. First, he said, the Japanese do not steal. Thus, their property has few locks or security devices, which saves millions of dollars each year. Most people leave their homes unlocked and do not lock their bicycles when they ride them to work!

Second, he told me that in Japan they do not eat when they are not hungry. When they are full, they quit eating. Most people in America eat, not for dietary needs, but for pleasure. He told me how this made a giant difference in his physical health, and how he felt good nearly everyday. He suggested that while I was in Japan, I should try Japanese food to see how I felt. I readily concurred.

That night we started my new dietary adventure with a nice meal at a nice restaurant. For the appetizer, six of us shared forty-five pieces of sushi. Delicious! They had squid, shrimp, and some things I did't recognize. Myself, I enjoyed eight pieces dipped in different sauces. After an hour of conversation I asked, "When will the main course arrive?" They asked me, "Are you still hungry?" I thought for a moment, then realized I wasn't. He replied, "Good! Because that was your dinner."

Every morning, we ate rice with small crab slices, or small pieces of shrimp and different sauces for dipping. For lunch we had a large bowl of soup with cabbage, a hard-boiled egg, vegetables, and thin slices of beef, and sometimes, small amounts of spices or kimchee on the side. For dinner we had a beer with more pieces of sushi. I never saw a salad.

Seven or eight days later, I went jogging and noticed a remarkable difference. I felt light and very much alive. All the fat and things that had held me down were gone. My thoughts had a new clarity. I felt like someone had lifted a giant burden from my body. What a wonderful feeling! The difference shocked me.

After returning to the wonderful USA, I immediately went to my favorite barbecue restaurant, ordering two full racks of ribs and pillaging my diet. Old habits proved hard to break, and I failed to maintain the diet I kept during my stay in Japan. While I still desire to feel the way I did, I have found no restaurants here that offer the small portions I grew used to on my Japanese diet.

I share this story to let you know that diet **can** make a great difference in our physical health and how we feel. We could probably all make do with less food. I truly believe that in America, we abuse our abundance of food.

HGH

In coming years, people will hear a lot about human growth hormone (HGH). In a double-blind, statistically significant experiment, results showed HGH to provide anti-aging therapy by affecting cells in the body and rejuvenating the skin and bones, regenerating the heart, liver, lungs, and kidneys, and bringing organ and tissue function back to youthful levels. Other benefits: after six months subjects saw an increase in muscle mass of 8.8 percent without exercise; they had higher energy levels; they lost an average of 14.4% of fat without dieting; their blood pressure decreased; and hair growth increased. It also removed wrinkles and resulted in younger, tighter and thicker skin. It improved sleep; increased cardiac output; created superior exercise performance. Cholesterol profiles improved, with higher HDL and lower LDL levels. People reported elevated mood and increased memory retention.

Never has anyone come closer to finding a 'miracle drug'. After scanning this list of benefits, why would anyone not consider taking HGH? I think that HGH is an important possibility for a healthy person. Because you can take HGH in multiple ways, and since too-large doses can create side effects, find a doctor with an open mind who could prescribe the drug for you in the safest manner.

Your doctor must know your current levels of HGH to find out if you need to add more. It might be possible to stimulate your pituitary gland and have normal HGH levels from age 40 to 60. You can do this with gland-stimulating drugs, which raise your HGH output. After this time, you may consider taking HGH supplements.

ENVIRONMENT

Did you know that our planet is 66% water? That our body is mostly water? When we drink water, it cleanses our system. It allows impurities to escape. It makes us feel better. Think of water as oil in the engine, the spark plug in the lawn mower, even as life in our body.

Most things we drink have low water content, or they package the water in ways that our bodies find difficult to process. Try to drink more water and less wine, beer, coke or anything else that might clog your system. If you can drink milk, please do. Milk might be more difficult for your body to process but the advantages outweigh the short falls. It has so many vitamins and minerals and other things that your body needs that it helps you. We surely do not know all the advantages of a glass of milk.

Air and oxygen affect our physical health as well. We know that professional athletes who participate in aerobic sports have a much lower rate of cancer than the average population. Studies were done with mice that show a positive correlation between aerobic activity and lack of disease including cancer. If you do not work out aerobically, at least do breathing exercises to insure you do not run short of life-giving oxygen. I noticed that when people get sick, it often occurs when they overstress from work or other issues. They are red in the face from lack of oxygen. I believe that the amount of oxygen we breathe controls our overall health.

Exercises:

Determine if you are sleep deprived. Go into a quiet, comfortable, dark room during the day or some time you would normally be awake. Sit quietly and remain still. If you fall asleep in less than fifteen minutes, you are sleep deprived. A person getting adequate sleep will take thirty to forty-five minutes to fall asleep. If you fall asleep each time you are on an airplane, or immediately in times of low stimulation, then you are sleep deprived. If you are cheating yourself of sleep, then you may likely be making poor decisions in your personal and business life. You will be functioning far below your potential.

List your two favorite ways to work out aerobically. Commit yourself to working out fifteen to forty-five minutes at least three times each week.

Find a partner to do your aerobic activity with. If you exercise alone, it is too easy to 'postpone' your workout. Don't fool yourself! You'll never get back to that workout. Losing your exercise will lead to diminished health and affect the other four areas of your life. Make a firm schedule and hold your partner accountable, and ask your partner to hold you accountable.

Questions:

1. Am I going to have an aerobic work-out three times each week for fifteen to forty-five minutes?

2. Am I sleep deprived? If so, what will I do to make sure I get enough rest and begin performing at a high level once again?

3. Do I get enough air and water? If not, how will I make sure that I do?

4. What can I do with my diet to eat less and feel better? What kinds of food could I eat that are lighter and more satisfying?

5. Who will be my partner for my aerobic exercise? What exercise is most appealing?

6. What are five things that will most improve my physical health?

7. Would I benefit from taking HGH to reverse the aging process, or do I need to stimulate my pituitary gland? What books or studies could I look at to make a good determination? I recommend "Grow Young with HGH" by Dr. Ron Klatz.

RELATIONSHIPS/FRIENDSHIPS

When senior citizens come into my office, they tell me how much they value relationships. In fact, the ones reporting that their lives overflowed with happiness and love were those who gave their relationships the most attention. People with good relationships seem very satisfied people. Having friends – whether they be God, your spouse, your parents, your children, your grandchildren or others – who support you and confide in you is perhaps the greatest gift you can give yourself. If you are happy with your friends, everything feels right with the world.

How can you develop relationships? The key is to listen carefully to what others are saying. Listening conveys that we value the other person and think them important and valuable. This basic notion seems to escape many people. They can't wait for the other person to end their story so they can try to top it with their joys or woes. If you practice the art of listening, friendships will quickly follow.

Names are so important. A person's name is the sweetest sound to their ears. But how many times do you forget someone's name mere moments after meeting them? Try, instead, to focus on their name – repeat it, maybe ask them to spell it – or play a word game with it. Soon you'll amaze people with your retention – and you'll move one step closer to making that stranger a friend.

We all carry a heavy load. Throughout the day, the people you meet will have just encountered a challenge in his or her life. Act excited to see them. Say to yourself, "This is the person that I will spend the rest of my life with!" You can bet, if this were the case, you would be interested in seeing them and very excited about what they have to say.

In today's world the stimulation and amount of information we must sift through every day is enormous. You can lift this load off a friend with a compliment and a beautiful, cheerful smile. What a difference you can make if you just empathize with the loads and challenges your friends deal with.

One of my friends focuses on special traits of the people he knows. If five things were going wrong in a person's life at the present moment, he would latch on to something positive and deliver a compliment. He is astoundingly popular! Everyone likes him and flocks around him. No one considers him particularly witty or cleaver. He simply finds something good in everyone he meets and points it out to them. If you can give this to a person, you will strengthen your relationship with them and give them joy and contentment. I think it is profoundly spiritual to see that people are starved for recognition! We all want someone to treat us well and recognize our achievements.

Napoleon first noticed that people would go to war and die for a military recognition ribbon! This tells how much value people put on recognition. In the Air Force, I saw how much people hungered for it. I served as the officer in charge of awards and decorations. Each time someone in our unit did something noteworthy, I would generate an award to make the accomplishment formal. Getting the awards made them glow with pride.

Recognize the people in your life. If you open your own business, set up a system of awards that will matter to your employees. This will improve your relationships with your employees and make a giant difference in employee loyalty and satisfaction.

One Great Model for Success!

In your network of friends, you should strive to have three special confidants. These three people will help you find success in your relationships and in other of the four areas. First, you need someone older than you are. This is someone who has gone down the road and can advise you in all areas of your life. You should find someone whom you can contact easily, who cares deeply about your success and will willingly share their wisdom. Often they are of the same sex, but more importantly, is someone whose opinion you value and who has experienced significant success on his or her own.

The next person is someone who is very close to your age whom you can call your best friend. Pick someone who lives near you, usually in the same town. This person cares about you, but is not necessarily more successful or wiser than you. Have him or her hold you accountable for the things you must do to grow in all five areas of your life. (And why not return the favor?) You should meet regularly with this confidant, hopefully in person but at least weekly by phone. This help-mate could be your spouse, but it might be a person unrelated to you.

Don't forget to give something back! For the third confidant, choose someone who is at least ten years younger than you, who has all the right material to make a difference with his or her life. You will assist this person in succeeding in their life by providing any support necessary. From this person you will get the joy and satisfaction of knowing you are a part of their life. You will not give this person a hand out but a hand up. You will teach them the secrets you've learned so they will succeed in all five areas of life. Prepare to learn even more as you teach, because when you give, you get more back in return.

A long time ago, a country in South America had a literacy problem. In that country, they asked each person to teach one other how to read. In less than two years they had significantly reduced their literacy problem. They succeeded with their motto of 'each one, teach one'.

If everyone in America took one person and made them successful in at least three areas of their life, what a difference that would make! We would have almost no poverty. We would be living in a different world. Share what you know and make a tremendous difference in their – and your – life!

One person that I saw practice this philosophy was Robert Calhoun, my Scoutmaster in Birmingham, Alabama. Over a period of thirty years, he helped almost a hundred young men earn their Eagle Scout Rank. Now, years later, these Eagle Scouts come back to his home and share their success stories with him. If only you could hear these touching and remarkable stories! They tell him how he made a difference in their life. I can think of no more most beautiful treasure a person could ever have. What a blessing! Truly, joy and happiness fill his life because he has made a difference.

MENTAL PEACE, JOY, AND HAPPINESS

We all know that we could gain success in the four other areas of life and still miss joy, happiness or mental peace. It saddens me to see people who have financial success miss out on happiness. One of the richest men in the world was Howard Hughes. He had every chance to have great peace of mind, yet he was one of the most miserable people in the world. One very wealthy person told me that being rich "was almost as good as mediocre sex." He admitted his disappointment when he became wealthy because he thought it would make him happy. It did not.

If you do not have these things in your life, you can start by faking it until you reach that level. You might start by writing about the times in your life when you had mental peace. What did it feel like? Maybe you felt confident and excited about the future. Try to determine how your life has changed, and if you can recapture that earlier peace.

Get up tomorrow morning and say to yourself, "Today I have happiness, joy and mental peace". Repeat it over and over. Say it fifty times. Your brain is like a computer. It will start to move you into situations where your affirmation will become true. Try it – it can work if you let it!

One of my favorite books, Think and Grow Rich by Napoleon Hill, covers this concept. It is probably the most powerful concept ever recorded: what we hold in our mind becomes our reality. Even if what we hold in our mind starts out untrue, the mind forces it into reality. It does this by first collecting evidence, then by introducing us to situations that support our beliefs. We feel greater confidence and energy as we move through situations that support the vision in our minds. Think about it! The mind acts like a *super* computer seeking out the knowledge, learning, understanding, people and situations you need to create what you dream.

Personally, to have mental peace, joy and happiness, I need to create the world's first positive radio station. A positive radio station plays positive music, music with a good beat and an uplifting message. It also has humor (The God within), and positive news about the people who are doing something extraordinary with their life. I see this as one of three keys to reduce violence in our society and for Americans to find meaning in their life. (The other two keys involve proper parental upbringing and a spiritual foundation.) When I think about a positive radio station I get very happy because I can see a world getting better with no effort at all. The people will hold positive messages in their subconscious, and their supercomputer (their mind) will draw them to this reality. What a beautiful, beautiful, beautiful concept! I hope I can pull it off! I will spend most of the year 2000 creating it. Listen for word of my endeavors in the news.

Years ago I passed through the lowest point in my life. I had gone though a divorce. My finances had been wiped out. I had very few friendships, and the future seemed bleak indeed. Depression filled my walking hours. I slept fourteen hours each night, stumbling through life in a perpetual coma. My dog, Hosehead, my beloved, dear friend would lick me as if to say, "You will get through this. I love you. I will stay here with you until you recover." It seemed like he was the only one in the world who cared!

The next day, I got up. On this particular day I really ached, emotionally. I felt that if I smiled, my face would crack. I said to the stranger in my mirror, "I love you, Alan Gay, and I will not live like this any longer." Pulling out a sheet of paper, I wrote down five affirmations. I remember them well:

"I love myself. I love W. Alan Gay."
"I have happiness, mental peace and joy throughout my life."
"My life is a beautiful mosaic filled with passion."
"I am happy!"
"I am financially successful. I earn $100,000 per year!"

As soon as I wrote these down, I felt a sense of relief. My face resisted smiling, but I forced one onto it anyway. I repeated these affirmations over and over until they came true! While it did not happen overnight, forming those phrases planted these messages into my brain, which took over from there. I combined them with prayer to increase their power, a topic we will cover later.

Find the things that bring you mental peace, joy and happiness. My dog, Hosehead, stayed with me until I got through my dark days. Since he doesn't behave well around kids, he lives with my mother in Atlanta now, but I honored him before he left by having one of my clients cast a bronze statue of him. These words grace the base of the statue: "Depicted here, Hosehead. It often brings looks of great amazement when people would ask, 'Is that really his name?' Skilled at chasing squirrels and traveling to exotic places like Vail, Colorado, and Alabama, Hosehead enjoyed people food and was very certain that he was a person. The one thing he could not figure out was why he had a tail, when the rest of the humans did not. This was because he ate people food and slept under the sheets. This tribute to Hosehead is to commemorate all of the high quality love that he gave. Some say that by just being in his presence, they feel more love and offer up a smile."

Exercises:

Ask yourself:
- ✓ At what time in my life did I experience the greatest mental peace? (Try to write at least five responses).
- ✓ At what time in my life was I the happiest? (Five responses at least).
- ✓ What things happened to me that caused my greatest feeling of joy? (Again five responses)
- ✓ What am I really passionate about in my life?
- ✓ What can I do to bring these four things (Happiness, Joy , Mental Peace and Passion) into my life? (Five responses please)

✓ What do I really believe I deserve? What are the things that I must create, or risk going to my grave with the song still in me?

Now generate at least seven affirmations that you can paste on your bathroom mirror and repeat every day. Use the affirmations as prayers as well. The power of the two together will help you achieve gains most quickly. Remember to repeat them until you have that in your life. Persistence that will pay off! Smile when you say them, and let them come into your life.

Summary Exercises:

1. Of the five areas of life, which are the most important to you right now?

2. Which will be most important in three years?

3. With these two answers in mind, how much energy can you devote to each area at the current time? Write down a percentage for each area.

Most people lose the will to live if they have no friends, no money or no purpose, and thus cut years from their life. If we make a commitment to always have these things in our life, we may live five, ten, or twenty years longer. What will we do with those extra years? Write down these answers because this is who you are at the deepest level.

CHAPTER 4

PRAYER AND AFFIRMATION USED IN FINANCIAL PLANNING

I promised in the beginning of this book that some things you would see would surprise you. Here we go! To benefit from this chapter on prayer and affirmations, you must keep an open mind. When I wrote this book just before the year 2000, most people were not open to the possibility of using prayer as the miracle creator in their lives. Few of the scientific studies done with prayer have been published in medical journals, or experts have ignored them.

Scientists don't like the idea of the power or the possibility of prayer. If you have an open mind, I will share a great secret in this chapter. I hope you are ready because this short chapter is really very exciting, and is a great part of who I am! I think you will find it the most powerful chapter of this book.

The best thing about prayer is that we can reach out and touch others and events outside of our bodies. You can affect others, positively or negatively, across the room or around the world. I deeply believe that to become a great financial planner you must master prayer. This probably surprises to you, since the importance of prayer is not taught and often ignored.

In my upbringing, I was taught to use prayer for spiritual or personal things only. No connection was made with prayer in our everyday life or for use in business. During that time, I never considered prayer as particularly effective, because I had not heard of the scientific data confirming the power of prayer. I saw it as something that weak people used when they couldn't make things happen through their own efforts. However, new studies on prayer have proven some very exciting things, and new worlds of possibilities have opened.

Numerous studies have addressed the medical profession, particularly with doctors or individuals that have prayed for their patients. In one instance, a group of patients that had suffered heart attacks or severe chest pains (strong enough to admit them to cardiac care) were divided into two groups. Patients in the first group had their names given to a local prayer chain, and numerous adults prayed for these individuals. Researchers gave no information was given to the people praying, only a request to pray in any way for these people. The second group had no organized action taken with their names.

After two months, the individuals in the first group had seen results only thought possible through a miracle drug. No one in the first group had to be put on a respirator. None were given any of the extremely strong drugs normally given for these levels of heart problems. (Some had to have mild drugs and other minor treatments.) Almost all completely recovered.

The second group had severe problems. Some ended up on respirators, as they could not breathe on their own. One passed away. Eighty-nine per cent required or spent time in intensive care in the cardiac unit.

This scientific study produced a statistically significant result. The only problem with this study is we cannot know if the patients in the second group had been prayed for. We assumed they were not, but we can not be sure. Because of this uncertainty, we can not rely heavily on this study as a benchmark for the effectiveness of prayer.

This study also highlights some ethical issues. Since the scientific community does not currently acknowledge prayer as a possible benefit, the ethical ramifications of its uses have certainly not been explored. It may be wrong to offer prayer to some people and not to others, even if under the auspices of a study. It would be similar to denying medical treatment.

To get around this, in two separate studies researchers introduced different variables and players. Christian Scientists conducted the first experiment, where the prayer participants prayed for microorganisms in one container and did not pray for microorganisms in a second container. In the first container, the microorganisms grew more robust and stronger, suffering less disease. They were superior in every way to organisms in the second container, which had 'typical' microorganisms from the standpoint of health. Again, researchers recorded statistically significant results.

Even with published results like this, the 'educated' (including the medical community) choose to ignore prayer. This may be because many individuals, educated and indoctrinated in the scientific process, have been taught that science is separate from things (like prayer) that defy logical explanation. Doctors and others do not consider it proper to suggest that prayer could benefit their clients. The facts suggest, however, that you can pray for your clients and make a difference with their lives.

Another experiment seems to me one of the most astounding studies ever done with prayer. In this study, scientists observed a computer which produced ones and zeros from a random number generator. In 100,000 examples, the computer produced the same numbers of 1's and 0's within a margin of error of 0.01%.

A single individual was then asked to pray for the production of more 1's. While he did so, the computer consistently produced more 1's than 0's. The same individual then prayed for 0's rather than 1's. You may have already guessed that the computer now produced more 0's than 1's! The computer produced between 10-15% of the prayed-for digit in each experiment. Researchers ran the same study again, with groups and individuals both praying. Results in both studies were again statistically significant and scientifically impossible.

While few are open to it, the fact is, prayer works. Knowing this, should you pray for your clients? **I suggest that it is malpractice if you do not!** It is like a doctor knowing a medical treatment for his or her patient and not giving it to them. You owe it to your clients to pray for them. You will make them stronger and they will make you stronger.

I try to arrive early at my office and pray for the financial (and other) success of my clients. You could pray for your clients to make more money, or to save more money, or to get out of debt. You could pray to keep their nest eggs safe from the IRS. Pray for them to have enough money to save, to tithe, and to work in their Hakuna Matata. (We will discuss the Hakkuna Matta again later.)

Prayer will enhance the other four areas of their life as well. Pray for them to have enough money to cover their expenses, and for them to have few budget-busting emergencies. Pray for their good health. Then end your prayer with, "In regard to all my clients, Thy will be done".

I won't go into great detail here, but other studies show that for your prayer to be effective, you must have "genuine concern for what you are praying for." You need not belong to a certain religion. In fact, scientific studies show that even agnostics who prayed got results. I only wonder, to whom do they pray? To whom it may concern? Of course this does assume that you believe in some higher power. Call it the love force, God or Goddess, or 'Fred', but it must be some higher being, doesn't it?

You also do not have to pray a certain way for it to take effect. You can 'request' pray or you can 'ask for intercessory' pray. Requesting requires you to produce a want list and ask for things by name. With intercessory prayer, you bring up a subject and ask the God, spirit or love force you believe in to provide the best possible result.

Despite the growing body of evidence, 'enlightened' people still ignore these results. Ignore them! You can pray for your clients and make a difference with their lives! Do it and feel the power. Just like The Force in the Star Wars movies, it flows through us.

Do not confuse prayer with energy! Someone might say to you, "I will send you energy next Tuesday when you are taking your test." This is not prayer. Prayer is just as powerful in the next room as it is on the other side of the planet. Unlike energy, prayer does not weaken as you get further away. In fact, this is the best part of prayer. The subject of our prayer can receive its benefits whether they are next door or oceans away. Prayer maintains its effect at any distance and it knows no barriers.

After you pray for your clients, you need to pray for yourself. When we pray for our clients we make a difference in their lives, and we should give ourselves that same help. To be as effective as possible, you must combine your prayer with affirmations. Affirmations may be a form of prayer, but they interest us because they remind us of our prayers and activate our brains to bring to us what we want.

I had a wonderful friend who once said, "Alan, you can have anything you want, but you have to know *what* you want. Once you know that, you can get it." I believe you can get it with prayer and affirmations. In fact, every successful firm or business began with a vision of what they could achieve. One of the most beautiful quotes in Think and Grow Rich by Napoleon Hill is, "There is nothing capricious in nature." This means that anything that you think of, you can have, because you would not have thought of it otherwise.

When you use affirmations, you activate the world's most powerful computer, your brain. Concentrate on your dream, and your brain will show you the path to take. Of course, you must be open to the path to which your mind leads you. Do not make plans too far in advance or plans that are too rigid. As the book says over and over, be open to all the possibilities that may lead you where you really want to go.

Let's look at some examples of how to combine prayer with affirmations. First, to decide what you really want out of life. Once you identify your dream, you implement a completely personal strategy to achieve it. This could involve praying for it two or three times each day. Use affirmations to supercharge your efforts.

Let's say you want to create a financial planning firm with 75 employees. You own and run the firm. Your firm makes over $10,000,000 dollars each year, and you take home a personal salary of $1,000,000. The employees work in a 32,000 square foot red brick building that you own free and clear. You have a yellow helicopter on top of it that you fly back and forth each day to your home. Your firm provides the finest services for financial planning, stocks, bonds, mutual funds and all types of insurance. You have nine accountants and attorneys on staff to assist you and your clients.

Congratulations on a very worthwhile goal! Think of all the jobs you provide and all the people you will help. You might pray for this dream several times each day, the more the better. The affirmation might look exactly like what we wrote in the previous paragraph, while the prayer may contain fewer details. You would write the affirmation down, or create a picture of it, and put it in places you would be reminded of it as often as possible each day. Remember, have a picture, write it down, and verbalize it as well. These three give you maximum chance to bring it into your life. I suggest that you have one affirmation for each area of your life.

Here are five possible affirmations for an individual. Notice that we have one for each area of our life, allowing us to progress in each area.

★   I radiate happiness, joy and mental peace to all I meet. I focus only on accomplishments, achievements, health and happiness when I open my mouth.

★   I make $70,000 each year!

★   I honor my wife in everything that I do. I honor my three closest friends by showing care and concern for them, and by speaking to them at least one time each week.

★   I decrease my weight by eleven pounds and do aerobic exercise three times each week for fifty minutes each time.

★   I read the bible every day and attend church every week on Sunday or Wednesday. I meet with my friend to discuss spiritual issues and work on accountability.

Before looking at exercises, questions, and commentary, let us describe the best possible prayer and affirmation. This would be one that you can visualize, verbally offer, and write down, the more detail the better. Try to describe your desire relative to all your senses. Describe how it smells, looks, and tastes to make it much more real than a general description. Imagine how it will feel – sound – look when you achieve the goal.

Exercises:

1. Decide if you are going to pray for you clients. List reasons and do further research on the topic if necessary. Remember, withholding prayer from your clients, is like a doctor who withholds a treatment.

2. Write down your dream. Try to write down your dreams in all five areas of your life.

3. Write down prayers and affirmations that support your dreams. If you already pray, you may not need to write your prayers. However, you must write the affirmations which support your dreams. Try to draw it, write it, and record it on an audiotape. You can hear it, see it or visualize it. You then have no doubt about what your dream looks like when it is reached.

4. Write down exactly how you feel when you achieve your dream. Write down how it will affect each of your senses. How will it taste, feel and smell? How will you feel when it happens?

CHAPTER 5

ONLY 4 PRODUCTS NEEDED!

In this chapter we will show you how to meet many of your clients' needs using only four financial products. The products provide long term benefits and can change your life and the life of your client. When you read the chapter on financial independence and multi-generational wealth transfer, you will see a detailed discussion on client behavior, which cuts to the essence of what a financial planner does.

What products do you need to apply this strategy? You can meet meet your client's goals with only four products. This may seem unusual because you will want to do all things for all people, but these few products alone can make a great difference. For now let us master these products, then focus your service around them. Later you will convert your products and services to an experience.

What excites me the most about financial planning is the incremental growth. I got discouraged about working for a big company when I realized that, after years and years of service to that company, I could be forced to leave and start over again. In financial planning you will likely notice an incremental jump in income for you and your clients each year. This is so wonderful. The security of regular growth and never having to start over are truly the best parts of the business.

If you go into financial planning, orient yourself toward the best results for your clients. *Do not get involved in anything short term.* One of the biggest mistakes financial planners make is getting involved with or promising clients a short-term (under three year) return. Your work and value to your clients is based on long-term returns. So many times, financial planners hurt their reputation and destroy their own mental peace by working with a client based on a short-term need. If their needs are for their young children's education or for retirement or for funding their values, then you can help! After you learn the client's goals, hope, dreams and fears and compare this to their values, you can provide them with a path to success. This will make a giant difference in their life, of which you will forever be a part.

Before we discuss the products, let's look at how to apply them. I repeat the investor's mantra: buy low and sell high! Unfortunately, many of your clients will seem to hide out, thinking of ways to subvert your strategy. The energy and effort my clients put forth to buy high and sell low amazes me. It almost seems like they consciously try to destroy their own financial plan. Let me give you a few examples:

1) A man calls my office and asks, "Have your heard about XYZ mutual fund? It paid 79% last year. I want to get on their bandwagon!" After researching, I discovered that fund had returned 16.9% for the last five years and 17.3% for the last ten. In a very high percentage of cases, a fund bearing high returns in any given year will then retreat to get back to its average return. The fund has an average performance that will require negative returns to achieve after a year like this. I told my client that he could not pick a worse possible time to buy this mutual fund! Statistics almost guaranteed he would buy high and sell low. By the way, the fund actually dropped 21.1% over the next year and 46.4% over the next three years.

2) After a dramatic three month downturn due to a small war in the Middle East, a client who had invested $105,000 called to complain about her bad investments. "I want to cash out and put my money in a CD," she said. I talked her out of her rash move, to her later pleasure. In another 3½ years, the value of her account grew by $62,000 to $167,000. She had forgotten that stocks do not go up every quarter!

You must educate each client on long term investing. This means they must learn to put more money into investments when the market is down. Clients must never cash out of funds when the market is down. In my own account, I increase my monthly deposit every time the market drops more than 1%. I look at the fund or the stock that went down the most and buy it. The only time I ever take money out of the market is when the market or the fund I am investing in hits a new high. So, convince your clients to invest in the market every month. Tell them you will call them when the market is down and ask them to add to their account over and above what they normally put in.

3) A client said that his Jaguar was old and he needed a new one right away. He had invested $397,000 through me, and his account tallied $386,500 three months later. I told him that, if necessary, he should take money from the bond funds or from his money market account to buy his car because these funds were worth more than he had paid for them. However, I encourage him to wait because the market was down because of the Asia Crisis. He agreed to hold off a few months for his new Jaguar. By the following May, his account had grown to $413,600 with big gains in his US large growth and technology stocks. He took out $61,000 equally from the US large growth stocks and technology stocks and left the large value and the smallcap stocks alone, which had not grown since his initial deposit.

This is a good example of buying low and selling high, since at least $15,000 of the $61,000 car cost was interest.

Now let's look at what you have waited for, the four products that can meet almost all of your client's needs:

- A portfolio with 8 to 10 of the best stocks in the United States.
- Variable Life Insurance-This product is so important and key to your client's success that an entire chapter (chapter 2) has been devoted to it.
- Indexcd Annuities.
- Variable Annuities.

These four products can give you the highest probability of achieving financial success for your clients.

INVESTMENT 1: *Stock Portfolio.* A portfolio of 8-10 stocks is very useful for clients who like to own individual stocks. Pick stocks, usually from the Dow Jones 30 industrials, which include the largest industrial companies in the United States. These stocks can be outstanding long term investments, and can do well in an up or down market.

At my firm, we choose stocks based on information from three sources. First, we discuss matters with mutual fund managers. Often a successful fund manager will say, "If I could only buy ten stocks, these are what I would have." Since successful mutual funds often contain 140 or more stocks, you may consider these ten as the cream of the crop. Keep in mind that he may mention stocks that, due to limits on what the fund can own, he can not buy for his fund.

Second, we pick stocks based on industry knowledge. Being in the financial services business, I have a strong sense that Jefferson Pilot Financial and ITT Hartford would do well.

Last, you may use the proven method of looking at the Dow Jones 30 and comparing the price-to-earning (P/E) ratio of those companies. This can give you a great list of companies that, being temporarily down on their luck, could prove a great bargain. To get this information, simply list the companies and compare the ratio of price to earnings for stock for that year. If any of these stocks are on the list you collected from mutual fund managers, consider it a very good buy. Be sure to update this list every year and make changes accordingly.

For 1999, our firm's stock list included stocks from Southern Company, ITT Hartford (HLI is the market symbol), Jefferson Pilot Financial, Chevron, Coke, Exxon, Microsoft, Starbucks, Four Seasons, JP Morgan, Sears, GM, and 3M.

Note that we compiled this list using all three of the above criteria. Except for Microsoft, this list does not include any Internet stocks, technology IPO stocks, and general technology stocks. These stocks are indeed worthy of note, and mutual funds specializing in this area offer a wonderful possibility. When telephones first came out, these stocks skyrocketed for three to five years before competition brought their returns back to sustainable levels. Like the phone companies in their early days, these industry stocks could also boom. Thus, carefully consider mutual funds in this area, but take caution in picking individual stocks. I recommend you use these to dollar cost average into on a consistent basis.

One client came into our office and had us invest $500/month evenly into the three sectors mentioned above. After three years the client had deposited less than $20,000, but had an account valued over $62,000! Can you imagine his excitement?

Having your clients hold stocks benefits you in two ways. First, your flexibility may give you an advantage over mutual funds. Many fund managers tell me,"The funds have gotten so large I am limited on certain stocks I can buy. If only I could buy more of these winners ..." By purchasing individual stocks for your clients, you have time-tested, proven winners that can really do well in the long term. With these, your client can benefit from the pride of ownership along with having a name brand.

The fees for buying and selling stocks can be higher than buying mutual funds, but with good long-term performance you can recoup your money. The reason these stocks excel has to do with their market position and ability to continually produce excellent results.

Stocks also offer you the opportunity to charge management fees to the client. This promotes a long-term relationship with the client and allows you to benefit from constant growth in a managed account.

USES 1. If the client wants to invest money for the long term (more than five years), but may need some of the money within three years, or may be anxious to see at least some short term gains. Put the long-term money in the stocks listed here and the money needed in three years in the money market and a bond mutual fund. These stocks can be mixed with mutual funds to get the exact portfolio you want. These stocks will provide the engine to long term success that your clients look for.

2. When the client needs a superior long-term return. These stocks have a glorious past performance, and look better on paper than a front end loaded mutual fund. These stocks may far out perform a mutual fund in a five-year period and win you a very satisfied client.

While you can change any of these stocks, make sure the ones you replace can offer a superior market position. These stocks have some international exposure and benefit from the low taxes and interest rates in the United States in effect around the year 2000. You can find alternate stocks by looking at the largest holding of your favorite mutual funds. Fund managers would likely grab up more of these stocks if they were not restricted by the size of their mutual funds.

INVESTMENT 2: *Variable Insurance.* Please note an entire chapter was used on this tool because it allows you to convert all of your taxable investments to tax-free income, which also leaves social security tax-free. Stop and read this chapter now if you have not done so.

Remember that we use the Variable Insurance strictly as an investment and look only at dollars in versus dollars out. For comparison purposes we assign a value of zero to the life insurance death benefits, though in reality this is very valuable.

INVESTMENT 3: *The indexed Annuity.* I consider this one of the most exciting financial products ever invented. Since this product is not an annuitized annuity, you will not get a monthly check from it. You can typically convert it to one, but that is not its primary purpose.

This product is perfect for anyone who can not stand to see the value of their account drop, or if they are over age 59½ and will soon need the money from their account.

The indexed annuity takes its returns from the stock market index. It is very often linked to the S&P 500. When the market goes up the investor receives a percentage of the gain, but if the market goes down the client loses nothing. Several types of indexed annuities crowd the marketplace, each with its own features. However, you should choose your annuity only if it offers the two most important features: one-year reset and good payout rate.

Payout rate. The payout rate – the percentage of the market rise you see in your account – should be no lower than 60%. This means that if the market pays 10%, the client would get 6%. On an investment of $100,000, he or she would have $106,000 at the end of the year. Again, if the market drops the account would suffer no gain or loss.

One-year reset. This means that the market goes up by 30% this year with a payout rate of 60%, the client would see 18% added to the value of their contract. Of course, this gain depends on having the annuity reset (the gains 'paid out') every year. If the annuity is only reset every 5 years, it has much less value and protection to the client. Wouldn't you hate to see the gains from a 40% market gain wiped out if the market fell back 24% and 16% the following two years?

Let us look at an example. Assume the market performance over a three-year span shows the following results: Year 1: -10%, Year 2: 30% and Year 3: -10%. If the client invested $100,000 in the indexed annuity, the value of the account would grow as follows: Year 1: $100,000, Year 2: $118,000, Year 3: $118,000. Compare this to how much the account would grow after three years if with money directly invested in the market: only $105,300! This shows why this product is incredibly attractive to seniors. The client never sees a statement with a loss on it.

When you meet with your client, ask the risk question. Say, "If you invested $100,000 and 9 months later your account was worth $90,000, what would you do? How would you feel?" If the client replies, "I would feel sick, I would lose sleep, and I would consider killing myself," then put them into an indexed annuity. Mutual funds, individual stocks or variable life insurance invested in stock funds will not work for these kind of people.

USES: For elderly, for your clients' liquid money, and for any closed minded individual. If you have older clients with a CD, the indexed annuity is perfect for them. Think of the little old lady with nothing but cash in the bank, in CDs, or stuffed in her mattress at home. You've found the perfect product for her! If you have clients who will not need their money for many years, then put their liquid reserves into the indexed annuity. Important note: some indexed annuities come with a checkbook for easy accesses to the funds inside. This makes it the best place for the "gloom and doom" investor who thinks that the world is ending and don't want their money tied up. For instance, when this book was being written everyone worried about the millennium (Y2K) computer bug. Technophobes predicted havoc, and scores of people braced for bank failures and market meltdowns. (I predict that Y2K will go down as the biggest non-event in one thousand years.)

Each year someone has one good reason to not invest in the market, and these people buy into it. My favorite reason not to invest is, "The market is priced too high, the stocks P/E ratio are too high, and there are no more bargains. The market has to come back down."

I rank this as the biggest untruth of the nineties. The price of stocks is based on buying and selling. Today hundreds of thousands of individuals add to their retirement plan each month. These individuals, when asked, assure me that they will add to their plan no matter what. Whether the market soars, plummets, or stays flat, they will continue to add to their retirement plan. This constant infusion of money makes the market continue to rise. This investment influx did not happen twenty years ago, and it is a key trend.

The only thing that could make the market unsafe is if taxes rose along with inflation. The market has never performed worse than in times of high inflation and taxes. While taxes seem high now, they are low compared to the rest of the world. Inflation is in check and not predicted to affect us for years to come. In fact, at the time of this book we had entered a period of deflation and prices were actually going down. Our economy had not seen deflation in twenty years.

Let us review the key elements of an annuity. I recommend that you share this with your clients when you are discussing a fixed, variable or indexed annuity. Annuities are:

Safe-In the Great Depression, annuity owners did not lose a dime of their money. Some people who left their money in banks did lose their money.

Liquid-The money can be easily accessed subject to some type of surrender charge that usually ends after seven or eight years. Some come with a checkbook to access your money.

Protected from creditors-subject to state law, annuities are usually not garnishable and often excluded from bankruptcy proceedings.

High Rate of Return-Variable Annuities pay very close to their mutual fund counterparts. Indexed annuities pay about 60% of the S&P Market return; the fixed annuities pay a rate very close to the CD rate.

Tax favored-As a minimum, annuities grow tax-deferred. This means you pay no tax on the gain until it is taken out.

These are the five beautiful characteristics of annuities! I think they are a remarkable savings and wealth accumulation vehicle.

INVESTMENT 4: *The Variable Annuity.* The variable annuity is a financial ICON! It is one of the most exciting ways to purchase copies of mutual funds. Copies of mutual funds are called sub-accounts.

I like to use Variable Annuities in qualified plans! Many financial advisors do not do this. The reason I do (and that you should) has to do with rebalancing and because these copies of mutual funds will not soon grow too large to manage. These two factors together could consistently provide more than 3% extra return to your client's portfolio. To go over these two features, read the chapter on life insurance.

WHAT ARE VARIABLE ANNUITIES?

The College Retirement Equities Fund (CREF) first introduced variable annuities in 1952 to supplement a fixed-dollar annuity in financing retirement pensions. Today, variable annuities are used to supplement retirement programs such as 401(K) plans, defined benefit programs, and Social Security.

Variable annuities are often called "mutual funds with an insurance wrapper." A variable annuity combines the best aspects of traditional fixed annuity (tax deferral, insurance protection for beneficiaries, tax-timing controlled-income options) with the benefits of traditional mutual fund portfolios (flexibility in selecting how to invest funds, the potential for higher investment returns).

Already an integral element of many retirement strategies that combine employer-sponsored retirement savings programs and Social Security benefits, the variable annuity market is exploding. Investment planners and advisors recognize variable annuities as an appropriate long-term vehicle for accumulating wealth in equities on a tax-deferred basis. In 1997, assets in annuities totaled more than $800 billion dollars.

Variable annuity investors control their contract options. They dictate the amount, frequency, and regularity of their contributions, how to invest their contributions, and when to disburse the money. The investor pays a premium to the insurance company, which then buys accumulation units, similar to mutual fund shares, in an investment fund.

The IRS imposes no limits on the annual unsheltered amount an individual may contribute to a variable annuity funded with after-dollars. In other words, you can put in as much money as you can afford. This is particularly important when it comes to supplementing retirement assets beyond the annual tax-free contribution limitation.

The variable annuity investor directs those funds in sub-account portfolios consisting of stocks, bonds, or cash money-market funds. Diverse investment options make it possible to structure an investment portfolio to meet a variety of needs, goals, and risk tolerances. These investments may be managed by a mutual fund company or by an insurance company. With the important advantage of tax-free balancing, investors can adjust their portfolios at any time. This allows an investor's advisor to carefully plan and manage the asset allocation strategy based on changing needs or market conditions without worrying about generating current tax.

Unlike a mutual fund, an annuity does not pay out earnings or distribute any capital gains, so these compound on a tax-deferred basis. The ability to reallocate assets without current tax liabilities, combined with the tax-deferred compounding of potential earnings, makes variable annuities a highly competitive investment vehicle.

A variable annuity's rate of return is determined by the performance of the investments selected. As the value of the stocks in the portfolio varies, each unit will show its own growth or loss. Today's variable annuity managers, along with their affiliate mutual fund managers, seek diversification, consistent performance, and competitive returns by maximizing a portfolio's growth and minimizing the level of risk. Variable annuity investments are often balanced by investing a percentage of assets in the fixed-income annuity option to provide a less volatile investment return. These fixed annuity investments tend to smooth out extreme fluctuations; investors won't profit as much from a good year in the market with such an annuity, but neither will they suffer as much loss of income during a bad year.

Payouts from variable annuities reflect the investment experience of the underlying portfolios. The amount of variable payments is not guaranteed or fixed and may decline in periods of market decline. However, if the annuitant dies during the accumulation phase (that is, prior to receiving payments from the annuity), the investor's designated beneficiary is guaranteed to receive the greater of the account's accumulation value or the full amount invested less any withdrawals and applicable premium taxes. Some annuities also offer *enhanced death benefits*, such as options that would enable a client to receive a step-up every six years to age 81 to lock in gains. (The step-up feature locks in growth at a designated policy anniversary, i.e. 6 years.) Also, in most states, this built-in benefit generally bypasses the delays and costs of probate.

Except in Pennsylvania and New York, states do not specify an age at which payments must begin from a variable annuity funded with after tax-dollars. When withdrawals do begin, only the amounts withdrawn that represent a gain are taxed at ordinary tax rates, while the remainder of the account continues to grow tax-deferred. However, if the investor takes funds from the annuity before age 59½, they must pay an additional ten percent IRS penalty on the withdrawal of any gain.

Variable annuities provide a variety of guaranteed payment options to the annuitant, that is, the designated recipient of the income payout:

▸ Lifetime income: The entire account value is converted to a monthly income stream guaranteed for as long as the annuitant lives.

▸ Lifetime income with period certain: Income stream is guaranteed for a specified number of years or for as long as the annuitant lives, whichever is longer.

▸ Refund life annuity. The entire account value is converted to a monthly income stream guaranteed for as long as the annuitant lives. If the annuitant dies prior to the principal amount being annuitized, the balance is paid to the beneficiary.

▸ Joint and survivor: Income stream is guaranteed for as long as either annuitant lives (for example, you or your spouse).

▸ Fixed amount annuity: Equal periodic payments are withdrawn until the account balance is exhausted.

The lifetime guaranteed income payout option insures investors against the danger of outliving their money and also offers continued tax control. Part of each payment comes from principal and part from earned interest. Taxes are only assessed on the portion of each payment that comes from earned interest (excepting with qualified contracts). Once a guaranteed income option is selected, the investor usually cannot withdraw money or surrender his or her contract.

Most variable annuities offer a free annual withdrawal provision that gives the investor access of up to 10 percent of the annuity value annually without paying any surrender charges. Any distributions in excess of that 10 percent are subject to surrender charges. No-load variable annuities that do not impose a surrender charge are 100 percent liquid but, like all annuities, may be subject to a 10 percent federal penalty for withdrawal of gain prior to age 59 ½.

Despite their inherent advantages, all variable annuities are *not* created equal. They can vary widely in terms of cost and available investment options. Because of their insurance benefits, variable annuities usually cost more than traditional taxable investments, such as mutual funds. There may be front-end charges (loads), management fees, and sometimes back-end surrender charges for early withdrawals from the policy. These charges and the length of time they apply to the policy vary widely across the industry. The average policy probably has a 6-7% first-year surrender charge that declines one percentage point per year. Some have "rolling surrender charges," which means that each investment you make has a new surrender charge schedule; for example, if you invest $1,000 every year, each $1,000 contribution has a new surrender charge schedule. I would avoid these, if possible.

In addition to portfolio management fees, variable annuities charge a fee to cover the issuing insurance company's administration costs and mortality and expense (M&E) charges. According to the 1997 Morningstar benchmarks, annual M&E charges for the current average run around 1.3% and are decreasing.

The higher the overall costs, the longer it takes for the benefit of tax deferral to compensate for those costs. A no sales load, low-cost variable annuity can help shorten that break-even holding period. In general, variable annuities are designed as long-term investment vehicles, so a break-even of ten to fifteen years may be affordable for investors with that time frame. Remember not to measure time horizon by when you will retire; measure it according to the time you would need to start withdrawals. Income distributions from a variable annuity are best used to supplement conventional retirement benefits or as a reserve until other payouts are exhausted.

The variable annuity appears to be answer the shortfall retirement problems of longer life expectancies and longer retirement periods. Current trends are leading to drastic and alarming reductions in expected pension benefits, as both corporations and government get out of the retirement benefits business.

WHAT IS A SUB-ACCOUNT?

A sub-account is a mutual fund portfolio held inside a variable annuity.

Variable annuities offer anywhere from five to thirty-five sub-account investment options. This number is increasing, and soon I expect the average company to offer fifty or more sub-account investment options.

Mutual fund account managers select individual securities inside the sub-accounts; the investor then selects the most appropriate sub-account based on the security selection for his or her portfolio. If this sounds exactly like a mutual fund, that's because it is. The same mutual fund (or "clones," as they are called) tends to have the same managers inside variable annuity sub-accounts; therefore, the same criteria exist for choosing a mutual fund as for choosing a sub-account. The same benefits, such as professional money management, convenience, economies of scale, and diversification also exist. Sub-account exchanges do not create taxable events and do not entail sales or transfer charges. Most companies do set limits on the number of annual exchanges (usually a maximum of twelve) before a transfer fee is charged.

The variable annuity, however, gives the added benefit of tax-deferred wealth accumulation. Sub-accounts usually include a list of the primary investment objectives, and it's relatively easy to determine what the fees are applied for. Sub-accounts must specify the primary group of securities held and the issuing insurance or mutual fund company.

The investment flow of a sub-account

All investment funds flow through the insurance company into the various sub-accounts, depending on those chosen by the investor or investment advisor.

Each sub-account has a specific investment objective. Combined with other sub-accounts, this gives the investor a chance for diversification and the ability to select different portfolios to meet allocation and diversification needs. Sub-account managers purchase stocks, bonds, or cash, which are valued daily as an accumulation unit, another name for fund share price of the mutual fund.

Accumulation units—shares—are purchased by the contract owner at accumulation value (AUV), without commissions, in full and fractional units.

Types of sub-accounts

Sub-accounts may be divided into several broad categories, These are:

- Asset classes seeking aggressive growth
- Asset classes seeking more stable growth
- Asset classes seeking low volatility utilizing fixed income bonds
- Asset classes featuring money market rates.
- A combination of these

Inside each of these classes, categories are further broken down.

Fixed-income accounts are established to decrease risk for those in need of meeting current income requirements. They include government agencies, corporate rate bonds, high yield foreign (or international) government corporate rate bonds, and certain fixed income choices.

Equity or stock investing would occur in funds for growth of principal. Since variable annuities are long-term investments, the equity sub-accounts will be the most important to review.

Other asset classes could include cash and cash equivalents, which would be more short-term. Table 2.1 illustrates the investment options available in a variable annuity offered to consumers through investment advisors. I have illustrated in the last columns the types of asset class that are represented. Remember that asset

71

classes are groups of stock with similar attributes that behave similarly during changing economic conditions.

You still may have questions about sub-accounts and mutual funds, how they work, and what makes up a mutual fund. The following section will address these questions. As you read it, think of a mutual fund and a sub-account inside the variable annuity as being the same thing. Although they are kept separate, and the funds within each cannot be commingled, for ease of understanding how sub-accounts work we will look at its predecessor, the mutual fund.

TABLE 5.1: SUB-ACCOUNTS

Small Cap Value	Capital Appreciation	Equity securities of small U.S. and foreign companies	U.S. Small Cap
Enhanced Index	Total return modestly in excess of the performance of the S&P 500 Index	Primarily equity investments of large- and medium-sized U.S. and foreign companies	U.S. Large Cap
Domestic Blue Chip	Primarily growth of capital; secondarily providing income	Common stocks of 'blue-chip' companies	U.S. Large Cap
Utility Fund	High current income and moderate capital growth	Equity and debt securities of utility companies	Energy
Money Fund	Current income with stability of principal and liquidity	High-quality money market instruments	Cash
High-yield Income Bond Fund	High current income and overall total return	Lower-rated fixed-income securities	High-yield Fixed Income
U.S. Government Securities	Current income	U.S. Government securities	Short-Term Fixed Income
Emerging Markets	Capital appreciation	Equity securities of companies in countries having emerging markets	Emerging Markets
Growth Equity	Capital appreciation	Primarily equity securities of domestic companies	U.S. Large Cap
Domestic Small Cap	Capital appreciation	Primarily common stocks, convertibles, and other equity-type securities with emphasis on small company stocks	U.S. Small Cap

TABLE 5.1: SUB-ACCOUNTS			
International Fund	Capital Growth	Primarily equity securities of companies located outside the U.S.	International Large Cap
Value Fund	Primarily long-term capital appreciation; secondarily current income	Equity securities of medium- to large-sized companies, primarily in the U.S.	U.S. Large Cap
International Small Cap	Long-term capital appreciation	Primarily equity securities of small and medium-sized foreign companies	International Small Cap
International Equity	Capital appreciation securities of small and medium-sized foreign companies	Equity securities of non-U.S. companies	International Large Cap
Small Company Growth	Capital Growth	Equity securities of small-sized U.S. companies	U.S. Small Cap

TABLE 5.2. Commission Schedule for a Typical Mutual Fund

	Sales Commission	as a percentage of:
Purchase Amount (A-shares)	Public Offering	Net Amount Invested
Less than $50,000	5.00%	5.26%
$50,000 but less than $100,000	4.00%	4.17%
$100,000 but less than $250,000	3.00%	3.09%
$250,000 but less than $500,000	2.00%	2.04%
$500,000 but less than $1,000,000	1.00%	1.01%
$1,00,000 or over	0.00%	0.00%

Class C shares typically have even higher internal expenses and pay the selling broker up to 1% per year based on assets. This fee comes directly from your investment performance. C-shares may have no up-front fee, possibly a 1% deferred sales charge in year one (sometimes longer), and higher annual expenses (up to 1% extra per year).

In Table 5.1 you will notice that the offering price is different from the net amount invested. The offering price, also known as the ask price, is greater than the fund's NAV (net asset value). The NAV is identified as the amount per share you would receive if you sold your shares.

No-load mutual funds do not mean *no cost*. Some no-load funds charge a redemption fee of 1-2% of the net assert value to cover expenses incurred (mainly advertising) and to discourage frequent trading. Buying a no-load mutual fund is like doing your own plumbing work. If you know what you are doing, you can save money; but if you don't have the required time and expertise, you can make a serious mistake.

Another important fact to remember is that when you call the toll-free numbers of a mutual fund company with a question, you answer comes from an employee of the mutual fund company and may give you biased advice. An independent investment advisor, on the other hand, will more likely give you an unbiased reply.

A qualified investment advisor does much more than simply select a couple of mutual funds for a customer. He or she takes the short- and long-term needs, concerns, and objectives of the customer into account and builds a financial plan. Investors who truly devote themselves to learning about financial matters and who follow financial news, reading enough to keep themselves well informed, may do this quite well for themselves. Most investors, however, do not fall into this category, and should seek professional guidance for their investments.

Asset Management Fees

Asset management fees, the fees paid to the sub-account manager for managing sub-account assets, are debited from the AUV and thus decrease your investment return. Because of the large amounts of assets under management, insurance and investment companies offer *economies of scale*, or competitive fee schedules, to their customers to offset this loss. The management fees charged depend on the complexity of the asset management demands. Foreign equity management requires substantially more research, specialized implementation, and transportation costs than the management of a U.S. government bond fund, and the fees will reflect those differences. Equity sub-account fees usually run higher than bond sub-account fees.

Pay careful attention to fee comparisons. Every dollar charged comes directly from the performance of the sub-account. Remember to compare the proverbial apples to apples – in this case, sub-accounts (see Table 5.3).

Table 5.3: Fees Comparisons: Various Sub-Accounts			
	Annual Performance	**Management Fees**	**Net Performance**
Foreign Equities	12.50%	1.25%	11.25%
U.S. Large Cap	12.50%	1.00%	11.50%
U.S. Small Cap	13.00%	1.20%	11.80%
Investment-grade Bonds	7.80%	0.65%	7.15%
High-yield Bonds	9.25%	0.75%	8.50%
Foreign Bonds	9.25%	0.90%	8.35%

Operating Expenses

Fees pay for the operating costs of running a fund. These costs can include employees' salaries, marketing, servicing the toll-free line, printing and mailing published materials, computers for tracking investments and account balances, accounting fees, etc. You will find a fund's operating expenses quoted as a percentage of your investment. That percentage represents an annual fee or charge. You can find this number in a fund's prospectus in a section entitled "Total Fund Operating Expenses" or "Other Expenses."

A mutual fund's operating expenses are normally invisible to investors because they are deducted before any return is paid, and they are automatically charged on a daily basis. Beware, though, that a sub-account can have a very low management fee but have exorbitant operating expenses. A fund that frequently trades will have more wire charges, for instance, than a fund that does not.

Transaction Charges

When an individual investor places an order to buy 300 shares of a $30 stock (a $9000 investment), he or she is likely to get a commission bill for about $207, or 2.3% of the value on the investment. Even at a discount broker, commissions will usually run between $81 (0.9%) and $108 (1.2%). A mutual fund, on the other hand will more likely buy 30,000 to 300,000 shares at a time! Their commission costs often run about one-tenth of the commission you would pay a discount broker. Where you may have paid a $0.35/share commission, the mutual fund would pay $0.05 a share or less. The commission savings can (and should) mean higher returns for you as a mutual fund holder.

MORE GENERAL INFORMATION YOU SHOULD KNOW

Dividends

Dividends and capital gain (the profits from a sale of stock) are paid in proportion to the number of mutual fund shares you own. Even if you invest a few hundred dollars, you get the same investment return as those who invest millions. Unfortunately, you have to pay taxes on these gains even if you reinvest them. With a variable annuity, you can defer those taxes until you withdraw the money.

Low Initial Investment

Each mutual fund establishes the minimum amount required for an initial investment and the minimum amount that someone can add to the fund. A majority of mutual funds offer low initial minimums, some less than $1,000. Annuities are similar, with minimums generally running around $5,000.

Liquidity

One of the key advantages of mutual funds stems from their liquidity. You can sell your shares at any time, and mutual funds have a 'ready market'. Additionally, shareholders receive directly any dividend or interest payments earned by the fund, usually on a quarterly basis. When the fund manager sells an investments at profit, the net is distributed, but the net losses are retained by the fund. Inside the mutual fund, when dividends and capital gains are disbursed, the NAV is reduced by the disbursement. Inside the variable annuity, the AUV is unchanged by the dividend and capital gains disbursements since they are not sent directly to shareholders who would subsequently have to pay a tax. For that reason, the annuity-sub account adds tremendous value to the consumer. Whereas you have to be very careful not to purchase a mutual fund prior to ex-dividend date (the date dividends are announced) when the NAV goes down, with the variable annuity, these dates are irrelevant.

Audited Performance

Laws require all mutual funds to disclose historical data about the fund through their prospectus: returns earned by the fund, operating expenses and other fees, and the fund's rate of trading turnover. The SEC audits these disclosures for accuracy. Having them on your side is like a vigilant guard dog trained on the people responsible for your money. Remember, all sub-accounts inside variable annuities are registered investments. This does not mean the SEC recommends them, but it does mean the SEC has reviewed them for abuse and fraud.

Remember that mutual funds do not escape share-price declines during major markets downturns. For example, mutual funds that invested in stocks declined greatly during the October 27, 1977, market crash when the Dow Jones plunged 554.26 points. However, the most unlucky investors that month had all their money riding in Asian mutual funds; some funds plunged in price by 30-40%. Widely diversified mutual funds took the smallest hit.

Automatic Investment

A major benefit of mutual funds is that you can reinvest dividends automatically and convert them into more shares. However, you would have to pay income tax on these dividends even if you did not use them. Inside the variable annuity, you can postpone these taxes. As a result, your funds inside the variable annuity compound, whereas investors in mutual funds have to ante up money out of pocket or redeem shares to pay the tax. In addition, investors who own individual stocks or bonds outside the variable annuity program must continually decide how to reinvest the stream of dividends and interest they receive. Take the typical example of a $10,000 U.S. Treasury bond that pays $300 interest every six months (or 6 percent a year). You can't buy a $300 Treasury bond, so the interest usually sits accruing in a money market brokerage account. This delay, possibly caused by the inability to invest, keeps saver from experiencing the magic of compound interest.

Switching

Most mutual funds offer switching, or exchange privilege, through family or umbrella plans. Switching from one sub-account to another accommodates changes in investment goals, as well as changes in the market and the economy. Again, in mutual funds this switching creates taxable implications. When you redeem Federated Growth and Income Fund and buy Federated New York Municipal Bond Fund, for example, you have to pay taxes on the gains you had earned inside the fund you sold. Inside the variable annuity, those gains are deferred until you withdraw funds from the annuity.

This critical difference benefits you, since new funds are constantly being created that you may want to add to your portfolio. If you own mutual funds and you decide to sell existing shares of one fund to buy another, you have to weigh the disadvantage of paying tax on the shares you are selling. I have met many investors who would love to further diversify but do not, due to the tax implications.

In both sub-accounts and mutual funds, the managers usually maintain cash reserves for redemptions. It's easy for a fund holder to exchange his or her investment for cash or for shares in a different fund. Some people say that annuity managers need to keep less cash on hand than mutual fund managers since annuity holdings are longer-term investment, and thus less likely to be sold. This idea does not hold up once you examine it. The managers have to worry about investors switching funds because no tax implications deter them. I raise this point to shift away from sales gimmicks you may hear and to get you to focus on the facts.

Flexibility in Risk Level

An investor can select from among a variety of different mutual funds, finding a risk level he or she is comfortable with, and a fund with goals that match his or her own.

1. *Stock funds.* If you want your money to grow over a long period of time, funds that invest more heavily in stocks may be most appropriate.

2. *Bond funds.* If you need current income and don't want investments that fluctuate as widely as stocks, you may want to invest in more conservative bond funds.
3. *Money market funds.* If you want to be sure that your invested principal does not drop in value because you may need your money in the short term, a money market fund or a guaranteed fixed interest investment may best fit your needs.

No risk of bankruptcy

A situation in which the demand for money back (liabilities) exceeds the value of a fund's investments (assets) cannot occur with a mutual fund. The value can fluctuate, but this variation doesn't lead to the failure or bankruptcy of a mutual fund company. In fact, since Congress passed the Investment Company Act of 1940 to regulate the mutual fund industry, no fund has gone under and none probably ever will.

In contrast, hundreds of banks and dozens of insurance companies have failed in the past two decades alone. These firms can fail if their liabilities exceed their assets. When a bank makes too many loans that go sour at the same time and depositors want their money back, the bank fails. Likewise, if an insurance company makes several poor investments or underestimates the number of claims policy-holders will make, it too can fail. However, insurance companies hold mutual funds and sub-accounts in separate accounts, keeping them separate from the company's assets. You can avoid debacles like the Executive Life problems (declared bankruptcy) in the early 1990s by investing in the sub-accounts of variable annuities versus the general account of the insurance company. If you do invest in the fixed-interest accounts, make sure that the insurance company is rated highly by all four of the major rating agencies: Moody's, Duff & Phelps, Standard & Poor's, and A.M. Best.

Major types of mutual funds

The number of mutual funds has nearly tripled since 1980. In the current universe of approximately 8000 funds, there are portfolios that suit most investment risk objectives. Likewise on the sub-account front, the number of options have skyrocketed, with over 1500 sub-account options available. One important note: Remember to analyze the funds available in your annuity. Since they may be available in other annuities, you should shop for the lowest price. There are funds which invest in high-quality growth stocks, or smaller aggressive growth stocks, or stocks that pay high dividends. Mutual funds that invest in corporate and government bonds are also available.

Most mutual funds permit customers to move from one fund to another within the group for a small fee as the customers' personal investment objectives change. Another great feature of the variable annuity is that, inside the fund groups, you can switch from Fidelity to Dreyfus to J.P. Morgan without suffering fees or taxes.

The company will state fund's objectives at the opening of the prospectus, indicating whether the fund emphasizes high or low risk, stability or speculation. Funds generally fall into one of nine major types: growth, growth and income, income, bond, money market, tax-free, metals, foreign, and specialized. The annuity sub-accounts will consist mostly of stock and/or bond funds. It would make no sense to put tax-free funds like municipal bond funds inside the variable annuity, since it is tax-deferred and munis are tax-free.

HOW A SUB-ACCOUNT WORKS INSIDE A VARIABLE ANNUITY

After you have written your check to the variable annuity, the variable annuity company sends the check on your behalf to an organization functioning as a *transfer agent.* Here your investment is recorded and processed, and the real safeguards come into play. The agent transfers the money, not to the mutual stock fund's portfolio manager (the individual or firm that makes the investment decisions, technically known as the investment advisor), but to a *custodian bank.*

A custodian bank – a separate organization – holds the specific securities in which a mutual fund invests, and keeps it independent of the mutual fund company. The employment of a custodian insures that the fund management company can't embezzle your funds or use assets from a better-performing fund to subsidize a poor performer.

Once the custodian bank receives the money, it notifies the mutual fund that new money is available for investment. The fund manager checks a daily account balance sheet and *new moneys* are invested according to the mutual fund's investment policy.

The Investment Company Act of 1940 required independent custody for each mutual fund's asset. This has turned into the key provision that has sheltered the industry from trouble for more than half a century. Independent custody means a mutual fund's parent company can go belly-up without any loss to the fund's shareholders, because their assets are held apart from other funds and apart from the parent fund.

Contrast this business structure with the far less restrictive setup between, say, individual investors and a real estate promoter, or investors and a stockbroker who may have direct access to the client's accounts. In any number of notorious incidents, individuals in such a position have taken the money and run.

The limited partnership of the 1970s and 1980s illustrated well a poor business structure. During these years, many individuals formed unregulated and regulated limited partnerships, and investors sent their money directly to the limited partnership company. An unscrupulous promoter could simply write himself a check. Therefore, financial scandals were numerous.

A money manager of a mutual fund has no direct access to his investor's cash. The fund manager only decides how to invest shareholders' money. The custodian who controls the underlying securities allows them to be traded or exchanged with other institutional investors only after getting proper documentation from the manager. The benefit of independent custody lies in making it very hard for a fund manager to use the money for his own purpose.

The Investment Company Act adds other layers of investor protection as well. Independent accountants must regularly audit every fund; a fund's board of directors, modern-day trustees, negotiate prudent contract terms with the fund's service providers and generally oversee the operation; and the SEC has the power to inspect funds and bring enforcement action against those that breaks the rules. In addition, mutual fund firms have legions of compliance lawyers, essentially in-house cops paid to make sure that portfolio managers, traders, and others follow the rules.

A Code of Conduct

Under SEC rules, fund managers are required to abide by strict codes of conduct. The codes require advance reporting of personal securities transactions to avoid any conflict of interest between a managers personal trades and what he does with his fund's securities. A manager otherwise could 'front-run' his own fund, personally buying or selling securities before the fund trades in them, to his gain and possibly the fund's loss. To avoid such potential for self-dealing—that is, favoring one fund at the expense of another—the SEC set down strict guidelines for trading securities between funds in the same company rather than on the open market.

How to read variable annuity tables

Both *Barron's* and now *The Wall Street Journal* list annuity prices. The first column is the abbreviated form of the fund's name. Several funds listed under the same heading indicate the total funds available within a specific product.

The second column, headlined 'unit price', gives the accumulation unit value (AUV) price per share. The AUV is identified as the amount per share you would receive if you sold your holdings. On any given day, you can determine the value of your holdings by multiplying the AUV by the number of shares you own. Remember to take surrender charges into consideration, since these are not listed in the paper.

The tables also help you to figure out the total fees that you pay in the sub-account. The last column lists total expenses, which consists of insurance and investment expenses.

Suitable uses of variable annuities

I have heard investors and investment advisors say things like, "I have seen the numbers and read the articles in magazines, but I still don't know just who should invest in annuities." This chapter will list the best uses of annuities as I see it. Not everyone will agree with this list. Most will say I am leaving out half of the market, and they may be correct. When I look at the fact that close to $500 billion lies in variable annuities and half of that is invested with qualified funds, I have to wonder about the decisions made by the sellers. As mentioned before, I believe in the investment of qualified money (like 401(k) and IRA) in the Variable Annuity.

Now I will explain in detail why I suggest these uses of variable annuities.

Nonqualified Systematic Savings

Once you have met your qualified funding limits, which for affluent investors happens very quickly, you have to decide where to invest additional funds. You have a hundred different options, but for long-term dollars, the variable annuity makes the most sense. If you have less than ten years to invest, use mutual funds; if you have ten years or more, use the variable annuity. Remember that if you have two investments and one is taxable, that one will accumulate less funds than the tax-deferred investment.

Time allows the tax deferral to overcome the negative aspects of an annuity, such as higher cost and potentially higher taxation at withdrawal. However, even though ordinary tax rates (charged on your annuity withdrawals) normally run higher than the capital gains rates on your mutual funds investments, your tax bill may not run higher with the annuity. According to a 1997 Price Waterhouse study of annuities and mutual funds, the majority of your mutual fund investment return will likely be subject to ordinary income rates anyway.

Lump-sum Alternatives

Investments in CDs, bond mutual funds, and high-turnover equity mutual funds have one thing in common. All, or at least the majority, of the investment return each year will be taxable to you at ordinary income tax rates. Ask yourself, "If I currently have investment dollars in these types of accounts and I am not using the investment income for living expenses, why am I paying taxes on it?" You would do much better deferring those taxes until you need the income. This is a no-brainer, since even the break-evens are in single digits. You would gain more in the annuity, despite the additional cost, after just a few short years.

Greater Diversification Potential

Many financial planners do not believe in annuity investments inside qualified plans. The tax-deferred annuity has a cost for the tax deferral, and you do not need that benefit in a qualified plan. Let's think for a minute about why you *would* want a tax-deferred vehicle inside a tax-deferred plan. The variable annuity lets you invest in as many funds as you would like, most with no minimums inside one contract. Therefore, you can diversify your holdings even if your investment is small. The added degree of diversification could very well more than make up for the additional insurance expense.

Another reason may be if you work with an investment advisor. If he or she uses Schwab or Fidelity as their broker, for example, you usually incur transaction fees for any switches or investments that take place. Inside the annuity, you are typically not charged. If you have $50,000 in an IRA and you or your advisor makes eight switches each year at $35 per switch, that would cost 56 basis points, almost the same charge as some of the low-cost no-load variable annuities. If you make more switches or have a lower account balance, the cost would be even higher. Therefore, the annuity may be a lower-cost alternative.

Asset Protection

What is asset protection? In certain states – Arkansas, Florida, Michigan, New York, North Dakota, Ohio, Oklahoma, and Texas – annuities shelter your money from creditors. If you practice medicine in Florida and you fear that someday a patient will sue you for malpractice, you may choose an annuity as a great savings tool. I recommend consulting a tax advisor in your area to learn more about annuities and asset protection. It could be the best place to put your money if you work in an economically hazardous occupation.

A Funding vehicle for NIMCRUTs

NIMCRUT stands for Net Income with Makeup Charitable Remainder Uni-Trust. It is a mouthful, but for those charitably inclined, it can be a great tool for leaving a legacy while enjoying the financial benefits of your investments. Simply stated, it is a charitable trust most commonly funded with a highly appreciated asset. You can sell this asset within the trust without tax implications. If you'd like to sell a stock without paying gains, consider this solution. You receive an income tax reduction for the gift based on several factors, such as age or income rate designation.

The annuity works so well as a funding tool because the NIMCRUT will defer your income until you need it. With some investments, like mutual funds, you cannot fully defer the income since dividends and interest must be distributed. The annuity, if structured properly, can fully defer income for when you need it most. In addition, the makeup provision gives you the ability to go back and get all of the money accumulated that you had not previously received. Again, I strongly urge you to consult with a specialized estate-planner, Renaissance TM, a financial planner, or charitable-giving attorney who is knowledgeable in this area.

Improving a Client's Existing Investments

Now you know the four products that you need. Remember that you need to manage client behavior. If you can keep your clients from reacting to gloom and doom and stay invested in equities, your clients win and so do you. With this strategy they will accumulate enough wealth to be financially independent and have an inheritance to pass to their children. With these products you won't waste time wondering if you have good products, and you can devote your attention to your clients' hopes, dreams, fears and values. You need not worry about the products because they will meet your clients' financial goals.

CHAPTER 6

THE PEOPLE AND RELATIONSHIPS YOU WILL NEED

Interactions with people will be key to your success and happiness. In fact, if you could develop the right relationship with just one person, you could finish your financial journey in one day. While that perfect business relationship can drive your success, we will examine that relationship in another chapter. Here we will look at relationships with your employees and people outside your primary business/customer contacts.

Let us focus on becoming a master motivator. Wouldn't it be nice if people sought us out for friendships? If our employees stayed loyal to us, giving us their best efforts? This can insure your success and your mental peace. People will treat you like a celebrity because they 'feel nurtured' when they with you. You will earn people's respect, and this will make a tremendous difference in your career.

Two examples highlight this theme. I had the pleasure of going to the University of Alabama, graduating in 1983. While I attended Alabama, Paul "Bear" Bryant coached their football team. In case you don't follow college sports, Bear Bryant was one of college's most successful coaches. Before he retired, he had won more football games than any other coach! When he died in 1983, so many people attended his funeral that most business and schools had to shut down, and many attendees had to wait 6-8 hours to reach the cemetery. In my entire life I never heard anyone say anything bad about Bear Bryant. What could inspire this much love and admiration for one individual?

He did three things for his players and the people who worked with him. I have noticed that people who become icons have a special gift of making the people around them become all they can be. When this happens truly remarkable things begin to happen. Maybe we can use this principle for our own success.

In the case of the Bear, one thing he did before a game was hire a private investigator to find out more about his players and their relatives. After the ball game, the Bear would host a one-hour TV show. If Alabama lost the game he would simply say, "There was nothing the boys could do. It was poor coaching and nothing they could have done would change that. I am responsible for this loss."

On the other hand, if they won the game he would show each play and make comments. These comments reflected the extensive research the Bear had done. An example: "There is Bill Rasmussen running down the field and putting us in perfect position for that next field goal. Since we only won by two points, you could say that his four-yard run helped win the game. What you might not know about Bill is that his dad owns a hardware store in Muscle Shoals and he gives over $8,000/year to charity. His father Tom has made a great difference with his life. It is no wonder Bill is such a good football player because his mother, Sarah, and father were such great parents. Bill also has a sister named Nan." Of course all the players on the team tuned in to the show.

Besides honoring his players, the Bear would also make comments about his employees. The Bear might say, "We could never have made a play like that without the skill and cunning of Jim, our offensive coordinator. Jim is a great asset to our team and everybody knows that, but you may not know that Alabama has scored over 815 touchdowns with Jim in charge. What a blessing to have him!" In short, the Bear never said anything but good things, and went the extra mile to find out what things he could make a big deal about.

How could we apply this to our situation? First, you need to have employees. A good rule of thumb is to add one employee each year after your fifth year in business. So if you started your business ten years ago, you should have at least six employees including yourself.

You may wonder why you need employees. You've done well by yourself so far. Hopefully, though, your business has grown, with more work to do every day. As the owner of a financial planning practice, you may charge (as an example) $600/hour when you are face to face with a client, giving a seminar or using the media. However, you can't charge a client that much to have you answer the phone or sweep the floor. Why not hire someone at a lower rate to do those tasks, leaving you to spend more time earning money doing what you do best.

In my firm we have done very well with this concept. As soon as an employee can pay their own way, I hire someone under that person to help with tasks not in their Hakuna Matata. This allows the person to pay attention to the tasks that excite them and that will make the firm money.

Each year we have a Christmas Party. At that party, we invite all of the employees' spouses, and share stories of their successes and remarkable accomplishments over a nice meal. The employees enjoy this recognition, especially sharing it with their families. The excitement builds each year because they do remarkable things that they know I will notice and share. This gets the employees charged up and excited about working for our firm for another year. Indeed, you can feel the excitement when I go over all the truly excellent things they did. We all love recognition, and this way we can give each person some of the accolades that they crave.

Lesson One: Have enough employees to get the jobs done, and emulate Bear Bryant, where every accomplishment gets pointed out in a public meeting.

Never point out errors in public! Your employees know of those anyway, so you can ignore most of them. They will tend to dwell on the things that did not work out, trying to avoid such mistakes in the future. It is your job to help them focus on their successes.

Using this line of reasoning, you should introduce a system that will focus attention on things that go well at the firm. Too often we focus on the things that do not work out. A case in point: one day my most talented personal secretary shared with me eleven outstanding events that had occurred that day! Each was extraordinary, and any of them could easily make her or my day. Shortly after that a fax came in from the Securities and Exchange Commission (SEC) demanding that she turn in a report three months earlier than originally requested. She instantly became upset. She quickly forgot the eleven wonderful things as she focused on the SEC letter.

In my 'Thankful and Grateful System', we spend as few as one to two minutes each day going over the events that went well. The system allows you to see what is going well in your life, and puts those not-so-perfect things into proper perspective. This powerful technique can make a tremendous difference in your office.

You can use the Thankful and Grateful System with your children as well. After dinner, have your children point out what they are happy about, what they are thankful for and what is going well in their life. Next, have them tell you the best thing about the family member sitting next to them. You will hear things you never knew, and you can truly appreciate the blessing you have. This gives your family a great sense of hope and certainty. I think it is particularly challenging for kids today because so many have no idea how they will fit in or what their unique abilities are. The negative messages broadcast by television and radio don't help matters, nor does the limited spiritual background and limited family support many children deal with.

Master the system yourself first, then point out the benefits to your employee. Offer the employees a gift if they follow the system for 21 consecutive days. (This is the amount of time usually needed to create a habit.) Offer whatever gift is necessary for them to do it.

In my office now, the employees focus on things and events that went well. They share a sense of success and pride in their work. Zig Zeigler once said, "Your attitude controls your altitude." This frees your employees to reach their highest altitude and become all they can be. But you need to work on this at first, because it is natural for you and your employees to focus on things that did not work out.

MAJOR ERROR: Publicly focusing on or talking about anything that did not go well. If the stakes are too high to ignore, talk to the person in private. If they do not excel at what they do and it does not excite them (no Hakuna Matata), you owe it to them to find them another position that they can enjoy and excel in.

Bear Bryant trained his players to be superstars on the field. As you can guess, the players performed at a high level, not only to avoid disappointing Bear, but so they could get recognition on the TV show each week. To strengthen his advantage, Bear had a special way of recruiting. Each year when high schoolers gained stardom for their gridiron efforts, Bear went to their home in person and sat with their parents and the high school Superstar.

He said, "You have the kind of game that we are interested in. I can not offer you a scholarship, but if you choose Alabama, as a freshman I will let you play in every varsity game. All I ask is that you play at your highest level." This excited a freshman, to play for Bear Bryant *and* to play in every varsity game their freshman year. For some reason, no other school offered this.

When the game started, the seniors and juniors would play exclusively in the first quarter. They knew they had to build an early lead, since the freshmen would play soon. Players approached it like the game would end in the first quarter. These juniors and seniors played at a very high level and with great intensity. In the second and third quarter, Bear Bryant rotated all the freshmen into the lineup until all had played for at least fifteen minutes. These freshmen may have lacked the skill, but they played at a very high intensity, hoping to become starters the next year.

Often the score remained close entering the fourth quarter. Now Bear could bring his seniors and juniors back in, completely rested and ready to play. Alabama's best players had rested for most of two entire quarters. They were ready to play. A tired opponent seemed to always play a fresh team.

This made it very hard for anyone to defeat Alabama and Bear Bryant, and very few teams did.

Lesson 2: Now that you have established loyalty with your employees, get your employees to become superstars. Do this by asking them to work only four days each week but paying them for the whole week. The extra day off will enable them to spend quality time with their family or go on a date with their spouse. Explain to them that they must do all their work in four days, therefore they must work like a professional athlete or entertainer and become a superstar at their job.

Make sure they do not work more than ten hours each day. Some employees may try to work more to compensate for the missed hours Friday. Don't let them! Tell them they need regular time off to become a superstar. Explain that they have to perform at a higher level and prioritize to get their work done. Of course, you must do this as well. You should take one day off and work four days each week as well. Never suggest to your employees that they do something you won't do. If you cannot work only four days each week, you will not get the employees to buy off on the concept. You, and only you, must show them it is possible.

MAJOR ERROR: Work your staff long, hard hours. This guarantees poor work.

MINOR ERROR: Not using lists. A list is essential for superstar performance.

MINOR ERROR: You or your employees working more than four days a week.

MINOR ERROR: Not taking one day every quarter for strategic planning. Remember: to work like a superstar you must have a list, work four-day weeks, take vacations, and do strategic planning each quarter.

I wanted to share the story of a good friend, the best 'people person' I know. I can find only good things about him. It seems that everyone protects him from bad gossip or character smears. Everyone talks about him in glowing terms – his friends, family, and business associates. I want to introduce Willie Kellum of Denver, Colorado. I spoke of him earlier in this book.

I bring him up in this chapter because of the intense loyalty he has inspired over the years. He used a very simple technique and applied it over and over. At first, I found it hard to determine just what he did, but later I realized that he used the same technique as Bear Bryant. After meeting a new contact, Willie would concisely and clearly point out an accomplishment or good trait in that person.

One dear friend of mine said, "Alan, all you really have to do is care for people and they will respond." Though this is close, I think it falls just short of the truth. Not only must you care, but you must communicate it as well. Now back to the master communicator.

One time I saw a person acting rude to another individual for no apparent reason. I thought that Willie would certainly let him have it. Instead, Willie focused on the man's recent raise and said, "I didn't know you got promoted! You must have worked really hard for that."

Willie's reaction shocked me! Still, to this day, I find it hard to believe what happened. The man grinned from ear to ear. He instantly befriended Willie, letting Willie see the best of him. He admitted that he was upset because his work had not been going well, and he appreciated Willie noticing his promotion.

Willie uses this technique on a regular basis with everyone he meets. He lets the other person talk first, notices an excellent quality or accomplishment and then simply shares this with them. Here are a few of his more famous quotes.

"Are those your beautiful children? They are so polite and well behaved! You must be so proud."

"What a wonderful idea! I never considered that. No wonder you've received so much recognition at your business, you are a very cleaver person. I bet your customers are very happy to be working with you."

"This is the most beautiful automobile that I have ever seen! What a wise purchase. No one deserves this more than you."

And my favorite: "I knew the first day I met you that you were going to be a big success. When you left my business I stood at the door and smiled, because I knew you were going to make it!"

After a while these things add up to make a big difference in your life and the people in it. The people around Willie all live up to the things he says about them. I do enjoy watching the flowers (people) bloom around him as each reaches their maximum potential.

Willie Kellum uses these over and over again, ignoring things that are not going well. He is a legend in Denver, and has reached incredibly high levels of success. He is truly a Denver icon and everyone wants to work with him. He combines Bear Bryant's technique with altering the agreement that we discussed in the first chapter, "Business is Pouring In and We are Not Sure Why". By using this incredibly potent combination, you can catapult your career to great heights and achieve incredible success. If you apply them both, you will be unstoppable.

We must still discuss a bonus plan, an exit strategy, and how to use our time. Since we need to do all our work in four days each week, we need to be very efficient. Every quarter you need to go away and plan your next quarter. No program does this better than the Strategic Coach Program. In this program, you learn one concept on how to improve each area of your life. You can focus on business or one of the other life areas, depending on your current priorities, but you can improve on the things that truly matter to you.

Since each member of the class is a business owner, you learn concepts and methods that work well in other business, along with concepts that work well in theory but fail in real life. These lessons come directly from business owners who have actually used the concept or technique in their business. Every quarter when you come back, the class will refresh you and keep you very clear about what needs to happen with your life! Call me at 303-306-6377 for the number of the Strategic Coach Program if you are interested. I recommend it as a life changing experience.

If you do not take the Strategic Coach Program, I suggest you set up your own time to escape the office every quarter to do your strategic planning. Strategic planning means planning to improve your bottom line in all fives areas of your life three months down the road. This is how you can achieve real success and gain mental peace in your business. You might set up a study group with others in the same business and meet together for a full eight-hour day once each quarter.

What will happen to your business if you do not complete this strategic planning every quarter? You will accomplish things that are urgent but not important. Essential task will fall through the cracks. You will move fast and do nothing. Soon your income will peak and you will feel discouraged because even harder work will not increase your income, and progress in other areas of your life will suffer.

This is the difference between working harder and working smarter. Your parents probably told you to work hard and reach your goals. This conventional thinking does not work in today's world. To work smarter, you actually need to work less, not harder. Please trust me on this as one person who has seen both sides of the 'harder and smarter' work ethic.

THE BONUS PROGRAM

"What is in it for me?" That's what your employees want to know. Reward their excellence by offering a bonus for superior achievement. Share the profit of the firm with each person involved in the bottom line. There are many ways to do it, but the only important thing is that you actually do it. At our firm we chart our fixed monthly expenses at a certain amount. For income above that number, the employees receive 20% of the profit divided among the employees who work full time. This simple program works for us.

Let us say the fixed monthly expenses are $40,000/month including salaries of the employees. If the firm earns $50,000, then $2,000 would be divided among the full time employees. This type of bonus program encourages the employees to work together, and inspect everything that happens in the firm, then make suggestions for improvements. Implement this program as soon as possible and make your employees eligible 4-8 months after starting at the firm. This kind of compensation produces much better results than health insurance, the 401(k) plan or anything given with nothing required in return. This will inspire those who really want to work to be a member of your team.

MAJOR ERROR: Running a firm without a bonus program. Show me a firm without a bonus program and I will show you unmotivated, lethargic employees that do not live up to their true potential.

MINOR ERROR: Make the bonus too high for the employees to easily obtain. Instead, make the bonus very easy to obtain. Change the bonus to make sure the employees feel that they can get one when they perform well. When they achieve it, laud their accomplishment and their skills and talents.

THE EXIT STRATEGY

How will you turn your business into cash? Much of your ability to work with business owners will come from your knowledge of this concept. Most business owners think they will run their firm until age 80. At age 80, while they still enjoy perfect health, they will take two weeks to sell their business for 90-95% of its value. This is absurd! It happens less than one time in a thousand. If the owner does not pass away or become disabled, they will still likely have a difficult time converting their business to cash.

As soon as you succeed in your business, think about an exit strategy. This means you must form a definite plan to convert your business to cash. First, you need a key person and a buy-sell agreement. The properly set up buy-sell agreement will peg the value of your business for estate taxes and accomplish your exit if you get sick or hurt (disabled) or pass away. Very exciting!

However, we want to plan on you leaving your business when you are in good health. Even if you love your business and excel at it, you still may wish to do something else after 15-25 years in this business. While you can accomplish this in several different ways, you might look at having a person to transfer the business to over a long period of time. If you use this strategy, have this person work by your side for at least two years. During that time you can get a sense whether or not things will work out.

You might set up an agreement where this person would pay for the business over ten years. It could be done by simple agreement or by use of an Employee Stock Ownership Agreement (ESOP). The employee might transfer some of his salary to an account for the duration of the buyout. During that time, you would transfer partial ownership, but would retain 100% control. You would transfer the ownership as the stock is transferred, usually when the business is completely paid for. If for any reason the buyer fails to meet the minimum standard outlined in the buyout, the ownership of the business reverts to you. After the buyout, it will be important to leave the business and let the new owner run it on his or her own.

I suggest you find someone you trust, and transfer or sell the business to them. Keep in mind that people rarely sell their business for a lump sum of cash. Even if you do, the new owners often require you to stay and work for 2-5 years as a consultant or employee. During that period, the proceeds from the sale of the business are transferred to your account. It thus behooves you to make a concerted effort to plan your exit strategy.

Many business owners could leave their business and do something else that equally interesting and exciting for them (one of their other Hakuna Matatas), and they would excel at that also. Not only does this provide more financial security, but it keeps a business owner from burning out. Thus knowing when to exit – and having an exit strategy – is key to your success.

In a typical lifetime, a person might complete an exit strategy and and convert his or her business to cash two or three times. Business owners very seldom do this because they have no exit strategy. I believe no one should work in the same business for more than 25 years just because of the boredom factor, and because there could be another career you could excel in and make your life more complete. Starting your next career when you have cash built up from the first one (or a lump sum) makes it a lot easier and less stressful.

CRITICAL ERROR: Fail to set up an exit strategy that contains provisions for death, disability or conversion of the business to cash while the business owner is in good health. Since most of us believe we will never die, we fail to complete these things. It is the same reason our clients fail to complete estate planning.

Exercises:

Answer these questions:

1. What work schedule will you establish at your firm? Can you find a way to get all the work done in just four days?

2. What strategy will you use to do strategic planning every quarter?

3. How many employees do you need and should you have now? What can you delegate to these employees the will give you more time to work in your Hakuna Matata?

4. Can you point out only the good and others and resist commenting on the other things? How will you do that? Can you use the techniques of Bear Bryant or Willie Kellum? If you cannot use these techniques, can you just keep your mouth shut?

5. What is your exit strategy? For Death? For Disability? To set the value of your business for estate planning? (The buy-sell agreement). For changing your business to cash?

6. How long will you work as a financial planner in this area of your Hakuna Matata? What will be your next Hakuna Matata after financial planning?

7. What will your employee bonus program look like? How quickly can you get it in place?

8. How can you institute the Thankful and Grateful system? What reward will you give your employees for completing the first 21 days?

CHAPTER 7

YOU NEED TO KNOW THIS!

What I like most about financial planning is watching money grow year by year, both your own and your clients. What could be nicer than seeing your income increase while doing something you enjoy? To achieve this you need to work with managed accounts and plans that pay you over a long period of time, and ignore any plan that will pay all your commissions up front.

With your clients, enter into this long-term solution that will benefit both of you. Summarize this arrangement by reminding your client, "If you prosper, I prosper. If you suffer, I suffer." No one could ask for more! How could your clients protest a relationship where everyone wins?

In our business the loaded mutual funds now offer C and D shares. These are mutual funds that have an expense ratio (annual charge) that is passed directly on to the financial planner. These accounts are powerful, as are the managed accounts. Give these special consideration, since they allow a long-term relationship with a client.

Why would you, as a client, want to pay a large up-front fee if you know that your financial planner has no incentive to service your account? Why would you as a planner want such an account? You have no reason to care about the client because any additional work you do for him, you do for free. Your only incentive may be to move the funds to obtain a second commission, which may not best suit the client. Try to avoid this situation.

In the very near future, all available products and services will use this long term pricing. This means that Variable Annuities and Variable Life Insurance will be available with this same pricing as well. I think this will revolutionize the financial services business, so the sooner you can bring this into your business, the better off you will be.

MAJOR ERROR: Working with products that only pay a front-end load or fees and pay nothing after that.

EFFICIENCY

If you have decided to enter financial planning, you will need to become very efficient. In any given day you will have many individual tasks to accomplish. First, you will need to find an efficient way to get your message out. I was very fortunate to have my wife direct the marketing of our firm when we first married, and she did a fabulous job at publicizing our service. In a clear and concise manner, she told our story in a positive, appealing and permanent fashion.

She first tried advertising in the phone book and other print media, with little success. Seminars on financial and estate planning gave us better results, and we grew slowly with referrals. My wife's master stroke came, though, when we approached Christian radio stations. Since we work well with those firms, we offered them a 30-minute show with clients calling in and asking financial questions. With this move, my lovely wife catapulted our firm into the limelight and increased our business to a level that I never thought possible.

These methods worked for us. You may find others more suited to you, either by following the paths others have taken or blazing your own trail. I do suggest that you start with referrals, always asking you clients for them and expecting them to respond (the power of the mind again). Whichever methods you use, become an expert – and efficient – at them.

TIME SLICES

Let's talk about how to best use your time. I suggest you break up your time into three main time segments. First and most importantly, plan enough free time. (Free time is defined here as time where you do not do any business related activities.) You should try to increase the amount of your free time by 20% each year. This lets you spend time improving the other four areas of your life, and gives you the time necessary to enjoy it!

Planning these free time days will give you a great boost of energy. This will add excitement to your life, always giving you something to look forward to. As soon as I finish a wonderful vacation, I can look forward and see the next one on my schedule. Because I like travel, I spend a lot of my free time on the road. However, I never overlook time with family (especially the grandchildren) and planning special family events like a 50th wedding anniversary for my parents! You should always be able to look to your calendar and see something coming up that excites you. If you can not, you are greatly limiting the quality of your life.

To enjoy your free time, you must work more efficiently, which starts with managing your 'stuff'. You know stuff – all those things that provide no meaning to your life or that you do not enjoy. For you, this could include changing the oil in your car, doing yard work, shopping for clothing, going to the dentist or buying personal hygiene products at the grocery store. In my book, these are mundane tasks that I am not paid well for doing, and that I do not enjoy. Call this time segment 'in-between activities'. You should plan for these in-between activities. Maybe you could schedule a day, once every 21 days or so, and 'waste' it accomplishing these tasks.

The other activity that we include in this in-between category, is getting ready for your highly compensated activities (your 'billable hours'). If you are planning a presentation where you could earn two years worth of income, you should set aside an in-between day beforehand to make sure your presentation is perfect. This may sound obvious, but unless you put it on your schedule, you may find the day booked with other tasks.

Rich people, of course, have found another way to dispose of in-between tasks – delegate any of these activities that they can. You, too, should consider paying someone to do these for you. (By the way, if you find a way to get someone to go to the dentist for me, please let me know. I will hire them!)

Your third time block I call the highly compensated activities. These are the activities in your Hakuna Matata that people pay you for doing. Isn't it great to make a great salary for doing things you excel at and you enjoy? For me, these activities include working face to face with a client, writing a financial plan, speaking to a crowd of qualified prospects at a seminar, or speaking on the radio. While at times I must do other tasks, I keep them to a minimum because they don't pay as well or I do not enjoy them.

Try to delegate other activities or just turn away from them. Refer small and problem accounts to your competition. Since your work is where you make your money and care for your family, I suggest that you only work when you can perform at a high level. If you are sleepy or have already worked too many hours, you can not draw on your brilliance and you will not make a lasting impression on discriminating people. You know – the ones that write the large checks.

To be efficient, you must make a list! I saw a poster that said, "Each morning in Africa a lion awakes and he must run faster than the slowest deer or he will starve. On the same day the deer wakes up and knows that he must run faster than the slowest deer, or he will be eaten." The motto I took from this: "When the sun comes up, make sure you are running." I would add, make sure you are running and clutching your list, otherwise you will, from time to time, run in the wrong direction, thus damaging yourself and your mission. If you do not now use a list, you will see a 30-40% increase in efficiency by using one. Note that these are all strategems to work smarter. Working harder is out. You will seldom see benefits by working harder; in fact it will keep you from peak efficiency because you are in a weakened state.

Stay away from all or nothing thinking! In my experience, this causes great inefficiency. Let's say you have a client that might invest in either of two different products, either of which would achieve a satisfactory result. If he chooses product A, you receive a higher commission. I suggest that you truthfully disclose as many of the benefits and concerns of each product as you can. Tell the client what other planners say about the benefits and concerns of each product. The client can make an informed decision about what is best for him. If you present only one product without mentioning his choices, you may alarm the client into all or nothing thinking.

Take the example of a client funding his children's education with US Savings Bonds, Life Insurance, Mutual Funds in an UGMA, Stock in an UGMA, prepaid tuition or an educational IRA. If you discuss only one of these, the client may question your objectivity and do nothing for his child. Thus, the child has no funds available at age 18 to teach him or her a trade. If you mention all of his options, the client then knows the risks and tradeoffs. You do not want to be known as a 'one-horse dealer'. You want to offer a variety of products and services in the most objective method possible.

If you had only presented Life Insurance as an option, the client's Uncle Bob (who detests life insurance salesmen) may encourage the client to do nothing instead. Uncle Bob doesn't care whether or not Variable Life may be the only tax-free solution for a child's education plan and may work very well. Thus, you must find a way to avoid all or nothing thinking for you and for your clients. Give him options! We share with our clients that they can do anything that will give them mental peace, but we are here to present possibilities and we have no preference as to which they use. You may have to tell clients this three or four times before they truly believe it.

CRITICAL ERROR: Pushing the client in to all or nothing thinking by offering only one possible solution to any given problem. Tell the client the possibilities, and let them decide. Only clients can make the decisions that are right for them.

Finally, you must get good market information and good advice. Remember that all you need to do is to have your clients buy stocks and hold them for at least five years. Every day you will meet with clients who have every reason in the world to fear the stock market. You must have fresh, up to date reasons why the market will continue to do well. Remind your clients that people constantly invest new money in the market. Because of this, the market will tend to go up just as it has since 1929. Try to help them understand that the market may drop temporarily, and that no one knows where the next 800-point change in the DOW will be. But you feel very certain you know which direction the next 8000-point change will go.

I want to suggest one more thing. "The market creates temporary losses, but people create permanent ones". It really is true that all you need to do is to hold for the long term and not sell when the market is down.

IDEAS TO MAKE YOU MORE EFFICIENT FINANCIALLY

✓ Run your business and family just like it's about to go broke. This means only buy the things that you "love" and "cherish" or will immediately impact your bottom-line. Do not buy anything 'nice'.

✓ Run an ad in the paper for high-ticket items. I had a man come in and offer our company a light projector new for $4,300. I ran an ad in the paper for this same machine and bought a one-year-old model for $300. Put the ad in the want-to-buy section of the classifieds.

✓ Instead of going on a vacation and paying for a hotel, try to trade homes with someone. A book called Home Exchange Vacationing explains this method. By the way, I suggest that you go on at least four or more vacations each year. This keeps you fresh when you work and lets you perform at a high level. This tip will let you do it at a low cost.

✓ Buy a car that is two years old and drive it five more years. The worst-built car sold in the US will still last seven years. Then you can sell it and retrieve some cash, while not spending large amounts to maintain or repair. Take the two-year-old car to a mechanic and have the car carefully inspected. Haggle on the price based on any repairs needed. (Most two-year-old cars will not need significant repairs.) Avoid leasing a car at all cost, as this is the most expensive way to acquire an auto. If you get emotional peace from letting your spouse have a new car, then go ahead.

To be most efficient, make sure your dream is big enough to give you goose bumps, and make sure you are excited about your life, your projects and who you are. Most people can not get a burning desire for their dream because their dream is not grand enough, or they believe themselves incapable of achieving it.

Vow to yourself to seek your success at the highest level, vow never to return to the mediocrity that you once suffered through. Make your life and your finances efficient today! Pursue your success massively and love every minute of this great privilege they call life. I have noticed so many people waiting for the last quarter of their football game to get serious and to put themselves in a position to succeed. Life is not a dress rehearsal! Today is the final act. So live with passion and find out what life really is about.

CHAPTER 8

THE FINANCIAL PLAN AND THE ESTATE PLAN
CHARACTER UNDER CONSTRUCTION

In the financial planning business, you will regularly receive a very valuable gift: your client's trust. Don't misuse that trust! Use your position to recommend products that meet the client's needs perfectly. This may sound basic and fundamental, but too many people forget it.

You will notice that people will take your advice on what they should buy. Within six-to-eight months they will know whether you have benefitted them. Once you have credentials, such as CFP, CHFC or MSFS/P, you can present a product in a way to appeal to any client. In fact, you can convince almost any client to make an initial purchase of a product. Do not be tempted to sway them into purchases that benefit you and not them! If you decide to travel that road, I can not help you, and neither can all the financial acumen in the world. If this is your path, your financial planning practice will fail. Even worse, the other areas of your life will suffer as well.

In the book <u>Think and Grow Rich,</u> Napoleon Hill says, "A building built on a weak foundation will crumble." This reveals the essence of what you need to succeed. I have referred several times to a class I take called the Strategic Coach. In this class they teach the four habits of referability. These exceptional rules state that to be referable, you should:

★ Show up on time.
★ Say please and thank you.
★ Do what you say you are going to do.
★ Finish what you start.

I have noted a difference between college graduates and non-graduates: a college graduate will usually finish what he or she starts. They've already proven that by finishing a series of projects to get their degree. I believe people prefer to hire graduates, even when they look for work in fields other than those for which they trained. It shows the importance of the fourth rule.

I know several people who seldom finish what they start. Maybe it never occurs to them to do so. Going to college, though, forces them to apply themselves, and to work towards a goal.

However, working with non-college graduates has an advantage as well. One advantage: they seem to retain more of their creative energy. These people, I have found, have fewer predetermined notions and keep an open mind to what is possible. Many of them think 'outside the box' very easily and have not been indoctrinated as to 'the way things should be'.

I think one of the most important things in life is gaining the respect of family and friends. This puts great satisfaction and pride in our life, and makes it meaningful as we grow old. You must make sure your client knows you recommended the proper investments and products for their own financial situation.

One product that can cause questions is Variable Insurance sold as an investment. First, Variable Life Insurance surely ranks as a good investment for a 10-year-plus time frame. In fact, the great return and the tax benefits may make it one of the best investments ever. If you sell it to a client, you must make it very clear to the client that it will likely have lower values in the first five to ten years than if they'd bought the same individual stocks or mutual funds.

In my own practice, I have noticed that the client assumes the money they give you will grow around 20% every single year. You need to give them more realistic figures, so the first sub-par performance won't discourage them. This is called managing client expectations. Show the client that the fund will be at its best right when they need it, ten years or more in the future.

Why not use a managed account or funds with no front-end load? The client will at least not be surprised by a front-end load after they have had the product for a year and have forgotten about the fee.

Next, try to invest your client's money at a good price. If a given fund just dropped by 3% or more, then buy into the fund as soon as possible. If the fund paid a 70% return for the year, after typically paying 15% annually, then do not put more than 5% of your clients money in this fund. It is folly to believe that the fund won't rebound, dropping back in order to achieve its long-term average! This is not a fund seeking a new level, like the stock market going from 10.5% to 18% average yearly growth. Expect this one very good year to soon be followed by large down years.

You can dollar cost average, but this usually will not give as good results as simply investing all the money. The main problem with dollar cost averaging is that after nine months of investing, the clients money will have grown very little. Most clients will not be OK with knowing they have not seen a return on their money when the market has gone up. Keep in mind that in the 1980s and '90s, the US stock market has risen 70% of the time and has gone down 30% of the time. Thus, 70% of the time you will not help your clients by doing this, especially if the market is engaged in a steady and predictable climb.

If you feel good about using dollar cost averaging and it lets you sleep at night, then use it. I do not use it or recommend it unless the market has hit a new high.

If a fund has just had its best year ever, I suggest you avoid it completely. You may wish to hold your cash in a money market fund until the mutual fund returns to a more realistic level, and then move the money into the fund.

If the client does not understand the investment you offered and is disappointed with the returns, he or she will not recommend you to friends and family. How sad, to recommend the correct product to the client yet get no referrals from your work. Now the client will cash in the plan and blame you for the poor results. Because of this you will not feel respected, which can hurt your morale and self-esteem. In short, you and the client have both lost.

For this reason, I suggest that you spend as much time sharing expected returns with the client as you do talking about risk. This is a totally different conversation, but I think it is just as important.

If a client moves their account for any reason, do not take it personally! You can learn from this setback. In fact, I would suggest that most reasons that clients move accounts have to do with them not understanding the risks or having unrealistic expectations in the first five years. Clients do not understand the market or the products you offer. Make it a top priority to explain these two key realities.

In my practice I have been blessed with the gift of trust. Most of the clients who meet me, for some reason, instantly trust me. After one year, though, they still sometimes forget about risk and expectations. If we have a person dollar cost averaging, they will often ask us why their account did not do as well as the market. If all the sectors went down, but the US went up, they may ask, "Why did my account not do better than the US?" I bring this up to remind you that you could recommend the correct product, and the product may perform exactly as it should, but the client complains about the results. Try to be as clear as you can with the client about all these things when you start working with them.

Another reason clients complain is that others give the client incorrect information about the product you sold him. This will cause the client to lose mental peace. Very often this information comes from someone who is not a financial planner and has never purchased the products you have offered the client. This can be the most devastating part of the business. This person can get a client to cash out of a superb investment to purchase something totally inappropriate, and have the client lose money or have it underperform. This person can cause the client to pay a fortune in taxes or surrender charges, but worst of all, this person can take away the client's peace of mind.

While you can not avoid this, you can at least ask the client who makes their decisions, and if they will consult anyone else about the products or services they purchase from you. After we do business with a client, I hand them my business card and say, "We are still accepting referrals. If you meet anyone who is retiring soon, will receive an inheritance or owns a successful business, then I would like to meet them.

"Also, if anyone ever makes you question what you did here today, please call me. Let this person come in so we can all three sit down and discuss it, before you take any action. I am here to help you and I want you to feel good about the things we do to create your financial independence and complete multigenerational wealth transfer."

While I believe in Asset Allocation – putting your money into many different places, such as dividing it between stocks, bonds, real estate, government securities, and money management funds – it is also appropriate to strictly offer individual stocks (or mutual funds with only stocks inside of them) to clients who have more than a ten-year time frame. Do not feel that you need to use an asset allocation portfolio with every client. The stocks are the investments that will create financial independence for your client. The more your client has invested for the long term, the better.

When you recommend a product to a client, show the client the worst possible case during the first five years of the plan. Ask them what would happen if this actually happened. Try to see what they would do. It is critical to discuss this, along with risk, before you implement a plan with a client.

MAJOR ERROR: Fail to explain the likely (short-term) results for a product you offer. Remember, the client trusts you as a good financial planner. If they did not, they would not have used you.

MAJOR ERROR: Fail to explain how to buy low and sell high to a client. Fail to explain expectations and risk to a client.

MINOR ERROR: Put too much money in the 'hot' stock.

To end this chapter, I would like you to consider being a total success at your business! What would happen if people got some urgency in their life and they became excellent at what they did for a living? I have seen so many people that are sad when they look in the mirror each day just because they do not excel at anything. What would happen to you if you lived today like it was the last day of your life?

Vow to yourself to seek your success at the highest level. Vow never to go back to the mediocrity of which you once were a part. Pursue your success massively and love every minute of this great privilege they call life. I have noticed too many people waiting for the last quarter of their football game to get serious. Life is not a dress rehearsal! There is no time to do it correctly later. Today is the final act. Live with passion and find out what life really is about.

CHAPTER 9

FINISHING SCHOOL

When I wrote this book late in 1999, my company, Southern Financial Corporation, had approximately one thousand clients. Of those clients, approximately half have no trouble financially. One thing that our firm does that other firms do not is poll our clients. I have learned more useful information from these polls than from any college textbook.

I have noticed that these five hundred clients do three things that give them an enormous advantage. In my experience, no one who does these three things has ever had trouble with their own financial plan. These keys – truly, the very heart – of financial planning are worthy of emulation. This could drive your success in financial planning. Let us look at the three areas.

First, they save 10% of what they make. This is of great significance, because while they are asleep they make money. They might have a statement that values their investments at the start of the quarter at $10,000. At quarter's end, the fund has grown to $10,353. At night, while they slept, the computer figured out the interest they'd earned. Not bad, making $353 while you frolic through dreamland. Note that the opposite occurs to someone who owes money on his or her credit cards. For the same balance of $10,000, the computer works overnight to calculate how much more you owe. You spent money while you slept. If you live in this great country, you can join either group – the one that makes money or that spends it while they sleep.

Set a good example for your children! We know they'll try to emulate their parents. If the parents drink to excess, the children have a much higher than average chance of becoming alcoholics. If the parents save money, the children have a much higher chance of saving. So, show your children your credit card statements or your investment statements, depending on which you have. You can teach your children an important lesson. Very few parents share these statements with their children, missing a great opportunity to educate their children. Don't lecture them! Just show them the evidence in print.

The second secret of financial success is to tithe to your church, or give to a worthwhile charity, 10% of your income. As soon as you start doing this, you will notice that you look at yourself in a different light. You are now a giver, not a taker. You will feel immediate mental peace about who you are and what you have become. You will respect yourself.

Where should the gift or tithe go, and what counts as gift or tithe? The Bible says give to the widows and orphans, to your family and last to the church. This is a good guideline, but I would say that you could give it to any charity that will use your money to make a difference. Give to a cause you deeply and passionately believe in!

What you give to your family counts as well as what you give to the needy. In my wife's family a wonderful lady, far younger in spirit than her 78 years would suggest, decided that she no longer enjoyed her work and would be happier if she retired. On Mother's Day we announced that everyone in the family would contribute something so that Grandma could retire in comfort. Tears filled her eyes as she professed her gratitude. I would suggest that any money that you give to your family or widows or orphans should count toward your tithe or gift.

Do not give your money to anyone who can make it themselves, or to organizations that will waste it. We constantly hear of bad-news charities, where 60%, 70%, or more of donations go to 'administrative costs' - i.e., lining the pockets of the shysters running them. As a good rule of thumb, a reputable local charity should forward a dollar to the cause for every $1.20 raised. Even a larger charity, which has much larger expenses, should still return $1 for every $1.40 donated.

Would you donate to a charity that only generates $1 of usable cash for every $3.26 it receives? Such a 'charity' does exist, and you have most likely sent your hard-earned dollars to them for years. That 'charity', which wastes your money on pork-barrel projects, stupid studies (Why do kids fall off tricycles? Why do inmates try to escape from prison?), and bureaucratic bungling, is the government via the IRS. According to two separate studies (neither of which actually completed, since the results bothered those in charge), the government's overhead consumed 70% of the money it brought in. Do you think you can find any charities which could use your funds better?

Consider this: Prior to 1913, the United States had only assessed income tax for ten of the republic's 137 years, and then only to help pay bills generated by the Civil War. For years the Supreme Court had ruled income taxes unconstitutional. However, Congress got around the courts by passing the 16th amendment and having the states ratify it. They accomplished this by promising to tax only the ultra-rich, leaving the average Joe alone.

At first, they followed their word. In 1913, at a time when the average citizen made $500, Congress taxed all income over $4,000 (equal to $60,000 today) – and charged 1% tax until your income exceeded $20,000 ($298,000 in today's dollars). Even as late as 1939, only 5% of the nation's workers payed income tax. That ballooned during WWII, reaching 70% in the following years.

What does this mean? A few sneaky politicians, seeing a ready stream of available funds, forgot their promises (and the frugality they abided by, when funds were limited) and soaked many millions of people. The rich, however, with numerous tax breaks, have largely escaped those taxes. So, you see, the IRS exists based on a broken promise. I hope you will do everything possible to limit the funds you send to this, the world's most expensive charity.

Note the benefits or blessings that you receive when you save or tithe. You will find that when you give, you get more in return. Many people already know of these financial benefits. I would like to point out that you also see benefits in spiritual growth, physical health, joy, mental peace, happiness and relationships. All of these areas increase when you tithe or give. Just think of all you get for only 10% of your money! Earthshattering, isn't it? I have never elsewhere seen such a wise use of money.

I will not share my ideas on why this is true, but I will tell you it certainly is true. I have experienced it first hand with our clients and with my own giving and tithing. If you make these decisions for you family, I suggest you consider these two questions very carefully: Will you save and will you tithe?

To do this you must learn to live on 80% of your income. This will challenge you, especially if you have already established your lifestyle that requires your whole salary. If you need help, I can recommend a wonderful book that examines two or three earth-shaking concepts. As far as I know, these concepts had never been published in any financial journal. The book, The Millionaire Next Door, shows the relationship between TV and out of control spending, also known as excess personal consumption. In addition to TV teaching our children to murder others and completely desensitizing them to violence, it also teaches us to exercise unchecked spending. Did you know that in 1999, when this book was written, the average person in the US spent $1.04 for every dollar earned? This of course makes it nearly impossible to save money or gift or tithe in any fashion. It seems the only money available to save, tithe or give comes from inheritances, gifts or other unearned windfalls.

While we are on the subject, this remarkable book also demonstrated that giving to individuals under age 40 actually lowers their net worth and income. Think about it – if someone can receive money for doing nothing, what incentive do they have to work? For a good example of how doling out cash rarely helps, just look at the old welfare programs. (While I always suspected this was the case, the fact it was documented and proven in this study is of great significance.)

It is key to note that money may be given to anyone under age 40 to help them learn how to earn a living. If we give money to our children for college, or to start a business at any age, we can help them on their way to success. If we give them money to buy a bigger home or to buy a car, we actually harm them. This the book calls economic outpatient care.

CAREER CHOICES

We need to share more about career choices. If a person could work in that special area of interest to them, they could excel at what they do, and if this area also excites them, they would have a great advantage that would effect all five areas of their life. This special area I call, what else, the Hakuna Matata. In the famous Walt Disney movie *Lion King*, this they define this Swahili phrase to mean, "no more worries for the rest of your days." I would say this ranks as the most important concept for the business owner and for people who want to achieve financial success. Only pursue a career that you can excel at and be very excited about!

Compare this to a 'job' where you work because you need the money, or you must pay for the lifestyle you've grown accustomed to. How sad, to spend one-third to one-half of your waking hours doing something you do not enjoy.

The main reason financial planners care about the Hakuna Matata, is because people who work in their special area typically earn raises of 10% or more each year. These extra dollars make a difference financially, giving people the chance to save, give, or tithe more. In summary, saving, gifting/tithing, and working in your Hakuna Matata are the keys. No one I've ever known who follows these three keys has ever worried about money, which let them focus entirely on the other four areas of their life.

How can we work in this special area? How can we teach our children to work in this area? There are two ways. First, you must ask yourself the following questions:

▸ If I only have two years to live in perfect health and then after 2 years I would pass away, what would I do for a career in the meantime?

▸ If I had unlimited money, what would I do for a career? So, if you had $40,000,000 what would I do for a living?

▸ If I could not fail and have any career, what would I do for a living?

Take thirty minutes, sit in solitude and answer these questions. This will give you a good idea about your interests. However, careers you have not heard of could interest to you.

For an alternate way to find your Hakuna Matata, take the Kolbe A test. This test will give an excellent list of 10-20 possible careers that are in your Hakuna Matata! You can Kolbe direct at 800-240-5202.

Nothing could be better than going to work in a place you enjoy, and you are excited about what is going on. It will be soothing, rewarding and very exciting. Going to work will make you happy! What a concept!

THE CHILDREN'S EDUCATION

We mentioned that you can help your children learn how to make their living. How can we educate them in the best possible way? In the past, security came from working for a large company. My father worked for a good firm, where they helped him with his education and gave him other benefits. When my father started at the telephone company, the average employee worked at a company for 24 years. At the time of this book, the average employee now works at a given firm for only 4.4 years before moving elsewhere.

If you went to a large company today, you would find their CFO looking at laying off employees to make the quarter look good on their bottom line. If you visit any small company, you will find a discussion or an orientation around retaining their employees. This difference leads me to a key point. Allowing employees an involvement and ownership in a small business will cause it to thrive in the future. Even employment at a small to medium-size business will create more job security than working for a large corporation with the down-sizing and layoffs that will happen in the next two decades.

Probably the biggest payoff with small businesses is the ability for you to work in your Hakuna Matata and have people around you work in theirs. This can give you great freedom to accomplish great things in your life. If done properly, you can convert your business from one person to a dynamic program where you achieve your hopes, dreams, values and goals.

The other advantage of a business in which you are directly involved has to do with the education it provides. A child might come to his or her parents and say, "I would like to start my own business rather than go to college." This could terrify them if they knew that only one in fifty new business startups succeeded. One should consider, however, the good and practical knowledge that accompanies running a small business. One may say that if a child were entrusted with half of their college funds to start a business, quite a lot of learning might occur, even if the business failed. Like college, the child is rewarded or punished based on habits and completed projects. (Of course, in a small business the rewards and punishments occur much more swiftly!) Since we are very interested in practical learning, this could prove very valuable, especially when compared to classroom instruction if the student is not ready for a traditional college education.

In the past I have talked to many individuals who have started a business. Even though many of them did not prosper, they say they would not have traded that experience. The lessons they learned about themselves and others influenced their lives and gave them insights as to what they really wanted from life.

ALWAYS ASK AND ALWAYS TELL!

There are several questions you should ask of every client. While this helps the client bond with you, it also allows you to find out what past experiences the client has had and how you relate to the client's values, fears, dreams and goals. You need this information to prepare strategies that the client will consider as possibilities.

Some very good questions to ask each client: What do you fear? What are your most important goals? To find out about their values, ask them what is important about money to them? What is important about what you can buy with money? In our society we exchange money for goods and services. Many things we really want and value are acquired through money. Ask that question more than once, until you get a long list of values. Ask the client what they hope and dream for. Ask them what must happen for them to be totally happy with their personal and professional life over the next three years.

Ask whether their parents taught them to save and tithe. What their parents did will likely show up in the client's behavior. If the clients' parents saved and tithed, then this client has an excellent chance for long-term financial success.

If you notice your client making unusual statements or holding strange attitudes about money, you may want to ask them their first or most vivid memory of money. One time I met a client whose a father had owned a business. One day her father's partner stole all of the money in the business and left town. The business folded, and her father got stuck paying the debts of the business. At age 12 she was forced to move out of her home. This frightened the woman, and led to great anxiety and apprehension about money for her. She was terrified to make any financial decisions and distrusted everyone. A person like this will need to work on these issues before a proper relationship based on trust can be established. These problems seem to belong to your clients, but after you agree to work with a person, they will become your problems!

In addition to deciding whether your client meets your standards of net worth or ability to save, you should insure they are emotionally well enough to handle finances. Since we'd like to help everyone, it's very hard to turn someone down. It is in everyone's interest to part ways while you still admire and respect each other.

After you have asked all of these questions, be honest and tell the client what you need to make the relationship work for you. You can set the tone for the relationship and get off to a great start simply by being real and authentic. The client knows he must pay you for your services, and surely wondered just how it worked.

PAYMENT

If you ask a client to invest on a monthly basis, make sure you know how they will pay for it. Of course, if the client has a retirement to roll over, an inheritance or money that is idle in CD's, then you don't need a strategy to pay for their plan.

If the client will pay for something on a monthly basis you, the planner, need to find the money for the client to pay with. If you do not, every time the client sees savings go to you, they link you with pain. One very good and simple way to get money for a client is to change their exemptions on their W-2 or personal exemption forms.

The best way to change taxable money to tax-free money is to elect rule 72(t) or rule 72(q). You can also use this to find the money for a client. When this is done, the money that comes out of the Roth IRA or the Private Retirement Plan (Variable Life Insurance) is tax free and does not count toward their social security calculation, possibly making it tax-free as well. Example: Let us say a client has $100,000 in his or her IRA. If they elect rule 72(t), it will give them approximately $9000 each year to put into a Private Retirement Plan. Notice that you 'found' the money so your payment did not impact the client's lifestyle.

Keep in mind that people find it hard to save because television teaches them not to. Our culture urges everyone to set their lifestyles higher than their income level. You can not force the clients to learn to save, and you can not revamp their lifestyle. You must find a way for your client to pay for this future.

It may be possible to take a loan from the client's current life insurance to start a savings plan. The client may benefit from this, as he or she can get money without sacrificing their standard of living. If you take this route, look carefully at the fees involved and compare them with the return you expect on your new investment. Very often this is expensive money for the client, so you must examine this transaction carefully.

CLIENT PRESENTATION

Believe it or not, your clients will have great difficulty understanding financial planning! Keep in mind that you do financial planning every day and your clients don't, so they have to exercise a new part of their brain when they meet with you. For this reason, when apprising clients of their possibilities, share everything with them in three ways: visually, verbally and in writing.

When this book was written, the two worst offenders of this rule were American Express Financial and Merrill Lynch. These companies provide a financial plan that is mind-numbingly long, with little visual and almost no verbal explanation. This is why the 15% of our clients that have used one of those services have come away unhappy with the results.

It is far superior to have a written financial plan that is very short and easy to understand. When you discuss it with your clients, verbally explain concepts while you draw pictures. Do not go to a new concept until the current concept is understood. I actually leave blank spaces and let the client calculate numbers of their needs for their children's education or for retirement. This powerful technique empowers the clients. You can use computer visual aids such as charts, graphs and bar charts, but make sure to keep them very simple. In many ways it is desirable to draw the concept on a white sheet of paper right in front of the client.

One of the greatest presenters and concept people I've ever met is Rock Gunther. Rock shows the client the three aspects of tax for a qualified plan and then for variable life insurance. He draws three boxes proportionate in size to the value of those boxes. He shows whether the investment is tax deductible, then whether the interest is tax deferred. Finally, the big box at the end shows whether the money coming out of the plan is tax free. When this book was written, only the Roth IRA and Variable Life Insurance offer tax-free money at retirement. For individuals, corporate plans are available.

ESTATE PLANNING

With estate planning, you can rocket your career to a very high level. It will provide great satisfaction and probably offers you the best chance to make the largest dollar difference for your clients.

Let's look at the better estate planning techniques. You can use these are techniques or ideas for your clients and family.

1. Good estate planning does not stop at paying the least amount of taxes. Estate planning allows you to leave the most to your children (heirs) and charities.

2. If you or your clients fail to do estate planning, when the husband and wife die, the family will likely feud over the assets. I have seen children quit speaking to each other because they felt they didn't get their fair share. Dying without a will (intestate) caused this. Here the estate plan, or lack thereof, created a family divided and not united. One brilliant person said, "Probate is a lawsuit against yourself, that comes due when you die."

3. One good estate plan is to simply keep your assets below the exemption amount ($650,000 in 1999, slated to increase to $675,000 in 2000). Use a credit equivalent trust to get the exemption for both the husband and wife and then distribute gifts until your estate falls below this amount. Keep in mind that, to do this, you must have the assets titled half in the husband's name and half in the wives name. Joint Tenant With Right of Survivorship, which causes all the assets to revert to one spouse when the other dies, will not work for this program.

4. The client's money can go to charity, the IRS or their children (heirs). Don't let the IRS have it! Clients, however, will not know how to insure that their children and charities receive it. This uncertainty causes such stress that the client will often not accomplish any estate plan because they can not resolve the hows and whys. One solution is to set up a family foundation. Have the money go to the foundation during life and at death. Have the children sit on the board of directors. The charities receive money now and then after the death of the donor. Have the children receive money only when they attend the board meetings.

5. No matter how bad a person you are in real life, you will be remembered well if you create a family foundation that continues after your death. You will leave a legacy that your children and grandchildren will remember. Most important, before you die you will teach your values to your heirs. Therefore you will have made a difference with your life.

6. Give your qualified pension plan assets away to a charity at death. This is the most taxed asset on your estate balance sheet. It will be subject to income tax (IRD-Income in respect of a decedent) and estate tax as well. It could shrink by 60-80%. If ever you wanted to give away an asset, do it here.

7. Use Charitable Remainder Trust, Family Limited Partnerships and Charitable Family Limited Partnerships to change the ownership of your assets. These plans allow you to change the ownership, but let you maintain control. Learn these techniques and practice them often. These can often provide discounts of 30-40% upon the death of the owner, and can provide a current tax deduction as well.

8. If a client has $1,000,000 ($1M) and they are earning 5% interest on their money, they earn $50,000 annually. This is very typical of municipal bond funds, CD's and money market mutual funds. Change their money to immediate annuities that will pay 10-25%/year. Use the difference to buy a 'second to die' life insurance policy to leave a large inheritance to their children (heirs) or to a charity, keeping in mind the possibility of a family foundation.

9. One actual example: an aged couple (he was 83, she a year younger) took a $1.2M loan against their $1.8M house, putting that lump sum into a second-to-die life insurance policy. The policy only pays a death benefit when the second person dies (usually a husband and wife). The payments on the new home mortgage would run $30,000 per year. In this example, both husband and wife had health problems which lowered ratios, and they assume the investments would earn only 10% annually, not 12% – which lowered ratios further.

Here is a list of the typical pay-outs for life insurance based on ratios and distributions based on age and input to the program. The 'second to die' advantage is great compared to regular life insurance policies. These are typical pay-out, based on a lump-sum funding of the policy at the stated age, for healthy individuals who are non-smokers.

AGE	RATIO
Male and Female Age 70	$1 gets $14
Male and Female Age 80	$1 gets $8
Male and Female Age 85	$1 gets $6
Male and Female Age 90	$1 gets $3

These ratios assume the mutual funds (sub-accounts) average 12% each year.

Note that life insurance is a valid investment. If I say that I will give you $100,000, let you invest it for 25 years in stocks, and then 'likely' give me back $1,000,000, this would count as an investment. If I say that I will give you $100,000 and you will invest it for 25 years in real estate, and then 'likely' give me back $1,000,000, this too would count as an investment. If I say, give me $100,000 and I will buy a 'second to die' life insurance policy that pays $1,000,000 at your death, then you should consider this an investment as well. The only difference is that the life insurance has less risk than the first two and might be guaranteed! Therefore it is superior.

Work out in advance how long the estate planning process will take. Tell the client you will only work with them if you can complete it during that period. It does not serve your client to let this process last more than 75 days. Let them know you will have to apply for the life insurance in advance so that it can be ready to go when the legal documents are prepared.

Work out the fees in advance. Get some type of retainer and then disclose to the client how you get paid. Do not hesitate to admit that you will be paid based the sale of the life insurance. Also, apply for the life insurance in advance. The ownership and the details can be determined later.

Have the attorney do his or her job in two months, or fire them. Remember that a person who hired a bad attorney has generated worthless paper. A person who purchased a bad life insurance policy has still increased the multi-generational wealth of their family, and made a great difference with their life.

For me, estate planning has been the most rewarding part of my practice and most important for my clients. I regularly ask myself, why did I wait so long to put it in place? I truly regret that I did not start it sooner.

To start estate planning you will need about $10,000 in savings. Commit to yourself to have one seminar every two months. Use the first $5,000 to run a half or full-page ad in your local newspaper. Advertise the seminar for people who have over $3,000,000 net worth or more. These are the one you can help the most. By the time you have the second seminar, the first commissions or fees will have come in.

Try to give the people who attend the seminar a beautiful resource book that has elder law concepts as well as at least ten current estate planning concepts. Our firm uses software called, "back office technician." Make sure you include at least five reasons why they should do business with your firm.

As quickly as possible, get an attorney on staff at your firm. Attorneys, as a group, can be disloyal and can confuse your clients. It will be confusing for your clients to meet with you, then drive across town to meet with an attorney. An on-staff attorney can make a difference and can join you in your office to agree with you and support the client as they plan their estate.

You owe it to you client to be efficient at estate planning. Read everything about estate planning you can find and become a genius. Be a recognized expert in your field. One of the best ways to learn about estate planning is the Million Dollar Round Table (MDRT). I highly recommend this great organization. They give millions of dollars to charities and make a tremendous difference in this world. Make sure you never miss a MDRT meeting – it is one of the great treasures in life!

CONCLUSION

I want to wish you well on your journey. While I will not be there in person, I pray for the people who read my books and for other financial planners. Know that I will be present with you in spirit.

I am excited for you, for all that you will learn and for how strong you will become.

You will be admired and respected by the people you help. You know there is something profoundly spiritual about those who help others with their money. This frees them up to work on the other four areas of their life, because they do not have to worry about their money.

Finally, I want to commend you for completing this book. I hope you did the exercises along the way and really benefitted from the book. If in the future you have the opportunity to learn more in a class or a book or a seminar, I suggest that you partake. You might learn just one idea or concept that will change your life!

In life, only a few things rank as truly important. I hope that today we find you at peace with yourself. I hope that you give back to your community and I hope that you have someone to share your heart. I hope that you have passion in your life and you are passionate about all parts of your life!

Most of all, I hope that you enjoy your journey!